POLICEWOMAN
was originally published by Simon and Schuster.

Books by Dorothy Uhnak

The Bait
* Law and Order
* The Ledger
* Policewoman: A Young Woman's Initiation into the Realities of Justice
The Witness

* Published by POCKET BOOKS

 Are there paperbound books you want but cannot find in your retail stores?

Policewoman

*A young woman's initiation into
the realities of justice*

DOROTHY UHNAK

PUBLISHED BY POCKET BOOKS NEW YORK

POLICEWOMAN

Simon and Schuster edition published 1964

POCKET BOOK edition published August, 1973

4th printing.........................April, 1974

L

Standard Book Number: 671-78330-0.
Library of Congress Catalog Card Number: 64-10653.
This POCKET BOOK edition is published by arrangement with Simon & Schuster, Inc. Copyright, ©, 1963, by Dorothy Uhnak. All rights reserved. This book, or portions thereof, may not be reproduced by any means without permission of the original publisher: Simon and Schuster, 630 Fifth Avenue, New York, N.Y. 10020.
Cover photograph by Carl Fischer.
Printed in the U.S.A.

This book is for Tony—
for all the reasons we both know, which encompass mutual love and understanding; and also because he lives my life as much as I do, and he knows all the things that I had to learn.

Contents

Introduction

I am a detective in the New York City Transit Police Department. If I were asked to state the most common reaction to this statement of identification, it would be the phrase, "But you don't look like a policewoman!" It has been a source of deep annoyance to me that for the ten years I have been a policewoman this exclamation has been offered as a kind of compliment, both by culprits confronted with the authority of my statement and by acquaintances in a less vulnerable position. A policewoman, apparently, is supposed to look a certain way: big, heavy, hard, tough, obvious. She is generally expected to wear her experiences on her face, to have them glaring from her eyes or resounding in her voice.

And then, too, I have been told that it is an amazing thing that I am in this work: that my training was in other directions—education, social work, to help and aid and assist people. Friends who have gone into these other fields suggest a certain polite disdain for my profession; acquaintances, upon learning of my job, feel it incumbent upon themselves to launch immediately into a bitter tirade relative to an unfair traffic ticket or an unprovoked show of authority by some surly policeman. Always, in their narratives, the innocent have suffered and been improperly served by the servant of the people.

I entered my profession as a twenty-one-year-old girl, dedicated to a job that seemed inexplicable to others. I would have chosen no other way in which to serve: my interests have always been in the field of human relations, in people rather than in products. In police work, I have been confronted with the raw material of lives different from any I would otherwise have encountered.

My education in life truly began, not in the classrooms of City College, but on the first day of my career as an active police officer. I had thought, rather tentatively, that I would become a social worker, and my courses in sociology, psychology, criminology and education were directed toward this field. However, police work had been in the back of my mind from early childhood when my heroes had been the real-life detectives of my neighborhood precinct. They had seemed, those detectives, to be in possession of all secret things, for they were constantly coming and going on unexplained missions to unrevealed places for unknown reasons. They seemed to me to be at the hub and center of all exciting and important events. I had watched them, envying all their hidden knowledge of the world.

When I noticed a small advertisement placed by one of the civil service preparatory schools relative to a forthcoming policewoman's examination, I felt that my future might lie in this direction, instead of in social work. And yet, instead of attending the classes designed to prepare one for the bewildering barrage of irrelevant matter that is characteristic of all civil service examinations, I let my studies slide, somewhat typically. I approached the written portion of the exam with a childlike trust: this was the thing for me and so I could not fail to do well. Instinctively, I would succeed. This complete faith lasted about three minutes—the time it took me to thumb through the hundred-question exam booklet. I searched for those questions whose answers I knew definitely, to get them out of the way; this would give me time to make educated guesses on the remaining questions. The questions were all multiple-choice, and the odds were three-to-one against me. I knew absolutely nothing about our city government or its charter, who is responsible for what, and which department handles what emergency. The seriousness of the situation finally hit me, but one consolation was the uneasiness of the others taking the exam with me in the large, school-smelly high school classroom in downtown

Manhattan. I got very involved in the questions toward the end of the exam: those badgering, tricky problems involving men doing things to roads in so many hours, problems that could be solved, probably, with no effort if you knew a little algebra. (I no longer felt smug about being probably the only student who ever attended City College as a full-time, matriculated student without fulfilling the mathematics obligation.) I had to draw long charts of numbers, count things out, and then, finally, take wild stabs at answers.

Comparing my answers to the tentative key answers published in the *New York World-Telegram* two days later, I found that I had achieved a score of 63, and 70 was the passing mark. But while marking the paper, I felt a strange burst of enthusiasm and a rather irrational sense of challenge: this job was what I wanted, had to have. The fact that I had written a failing paper meant nothing. In reading and rereading some of the questions and my answers, I started to argue against the choices given in the paper. Finally, I typed out twelve pages of protest to the Civil Service Commission—and probably the Commission has ever since regretted allowing candidates to take duplicate exam papers home.

The written examination was in April. In August, I received a stiff card from the Civil Service Commissioners telling me to report for a medical examination and a competitive physical exam in early September. I have always had a secret, warm feeling that somehow the Civil Service Commissioners held my twelve typewritten, single-spaced pages in their collective hands, caressing them like innocent hopes, kindly. Whatever the facts (perhaps some questions I had answered incorrectly were protested by other candidates?) I had passed the first part. I was not really surprised. I knew I would make it, somehow.

Once again, the small ads appeared: Prepare now for the physical examination for policewoman. This time, I did consider going to their gymnasium. I thought about it. But at the time, I was group leader for some twenty-two nine-year-old boys at a settlement house on the Lower East Side. We chased each other and swam in city pools and hiked on city streets all summer, so I was in pretty good physical condition. Weight-lifting was one of the requirements, so I practiced lifting small boys, starting with the lightest and working my way up to the rugged little bullish ones who forced their feet into the pavement, making me strain my muscles.

It was a hot, humid September day when I arrived at the testing place—a large open playground in Van Cortlandt Park in the Bronx. Overhead was the elevated subway, and near by was a group of red-faced workmen to cheer us on. The street was lined with elderly retired men, women with baby carriages and amused expressions, adolescents (apparently future clients, for it was during school hours) and, watching from behind a tree, my husband, secretly cheering me on, for God knows what reason, except that it was something that seemed really important to me.

I did fine in the running and leaping event: this was a wonderful sport from my point of view and so easy that I felt a vague guilt about it. From a flat position on my back, I had to scramble to my feet at the sound of a whistle, race around a zigzag course and through a barrel, zoom out, leap a shoulder-high barrier, swing back, and race to the starting point. I had been doing this all summer in pursuit of fleet-footed little boys, and I was an expert at dodging and twisting. As I leaped the barrier, a bright light flashed in my face. The *New York Times* photographer had been waiting for someone with an unorthodox leap: I did a johnnypump version, taught me by a nine-year-old—very different, but far more effective than what had been taught at the more proper prep schools.

The weight-lifting events were an entirely different matter. I stood watching the other girls, to learn how to lift the barbells over my head. I didn't watch long enough, however, for when I saw a girl about my height and weight walk up to the heaviest weight—about forty pounds—and heave it skyward with no apparent effort, I volunteered to be next. I made for the biggest one and got it to shoulder height. The object was to straighten it over your head, elbow stiff. I took a deep breath and fought it upward. The weight pressed back and my arm bent; the barbell thudded against the side of my head. There was a collective groan—of sympathy, and also of relief that it was me, not them. The tester was a very nice man (the brother, I am sure, of the man who accepted my not very logical written protests), for he called me over to his card-table desk and asked, patiently, where I had learned weight-lifting. I told him that I was in the process of learning right now, and he explained a little about shifting weight, stance, thrust, and told me to get on the end of the line and watch how the others did it. When my turn came again, he told me to pick the least heavy weight for qualifying purposes, and with some great effort, I managed to straight-arm it. I also managed the next best weight, and let it go at that.

The last was the "killer event." I had practiced sit-ups until my normally flat stomach was as hard as iron. Now they wanted me to lie down and lift a weight that was placed under my neck and shoulders. Some girls held my feet and there was a terrible commotion. My iron stomach suddenly became jelly: it was unwilling to bend, to pull me to the required sitting position. In a deathlike resolve (for I surely felt it was suicide to all my vital organs), with a terrible gasp I put my entire existence into one be-all or end-all effort: I sat up with the smallest qualifying weight practically welded to my shoulders. The tester asked if I'd like to try the next weight. I said no, I thought not.

My score was qualifying, but not spectacularly so. There were three miserable girls there that day, all long-legged and skinny, who had achieved perfect scores in all the events.

The next morning I could not report to the settlement house for work. I could not lift one hand off the bed: my body was a great massive ache from my shoulders to my fingers and toes. Tony, my husband, started off for work, then returned two minutes later with the *New York Times*. There was my picture—in fringed shorts, mouth open, tongue sticking out. I was leaping over the barrier like some escaping sneak thief. My picture was flanked by photos of the nonchalant one hundred per centers.

All in all, however, I did not do too badly. Or perhaps others did worse, or hadn't the heart for protest. Out of 1,240 girls who had taken the examination, 148 made the final list. I was number 63 on the list. I was happy, of course, to be on the list, but there was a nagging feeling, also typical of me, that I should have been number one. Maybe, had I made a greater effort . . .

The New York City Police Department moves slowly in calling candidates for the policewoman position. In December, 1953, I received a printed form requiring me to present myself if I wished to be considered for immediate appointment to the New York City Transit Police Department. I had never heard of the New York City Transit Police Department. I quickly learned that the salary, working hours and job were substantially the same as those in the New York City Police Department, and that upon acceptance of this position, my name would remain on the policewoman list for the N.Y.C.P.D., and that I would still be called by them in turn.

It was not with any sense of elation that I appeared for the interview, for I did not at the time realize that my future would be bound with this police department. When, a year later, I was called by the New York City Police Department, I turned the job down, for I had in a true sense "found my home." In the ten years that I have been with the Transit Police (whose job it is to police the entire transit system of New York City), the Department has grown from a rather small police organization supervised by superior officers assigned from the New York City Police Department, or "the street," as we refer to it, to a completely independent, modern, competent police organization of approximately a thousand members. It is the fifth largest police force in New York State and is larger than the police departments of many cities. We have our own chief and our entire upper echelon has been graduated from the FBI National Academy in Washington, D.C. I am admittedly chauvinistic about the Transit Police Department, for I was a member of the

Department during its growing years and am proud of its advancement in the police world.

Now my reader might ask why I chose to set this book within the framework of the New York City Police Department rather than the New York City Transit Police Department. Perhaps the first reason is that I am still employed as a detective by the Transit Police, and there is a certain natural reticence involved. Secondly, and most important, is the fact that police officers, regardless of their area of concern, have common experiences, common knowledge. One officer's range of awareness is identical to that of any other police officer anywhere in the world. The policeman inhabits a total world and can move freely in any jurisdiction of the police world with total understanding. Any policeman, anywhere, can understand the problems of any other policeman. The knowledge I have gained as a police officer with the Transit Police Department is no different from the knowledge gained by members of the New York City Police Department. I felt, as a writer, that I would have freer range to explore this world by moving from my own department to the somewhat broader area of "the street."

I am now assigned to the Special Services Squad of the Transit Police Department and work closely with members of the Department's top echelon. My field assignments are only occasional and not of a particularly perilous nature. They are, however, extremely interesting for the most part and of a highly confidential nature; hence, my present assignment does not enter into this book.

Before proceeding with my story and ending this informal introduction, I would like to answer some questions that I can anticipate from past experience.

One of the questions most frequently asked of me is, "How does your husband feel about your job?" I have worked with men who seem to measure their masculinity by the dangers to which they have been exposed, by their toughness and hardness, and by the dependency of their wives. These men have declared in no uncertain terms, "I'd never let my wife be a cop!" My husband is an electrical designer. He has never felt that any of my accomplishments in police work, nor any of the ensuing publicity—the newspaper stories and television appearances and departmental honors—have taken anything from him, or detracted from his self-image as a man. Rather, they have enhanced his sense of pride in me and enriched our relationship as man and wife. His complete confidence in my ability to cope with whatever came along has been the real source of my strength in the face of difficult events, and it has been unwavering and steady and true. Tony has told me many times throughout the thirteen years of our marriage, that my career in police work has given me a maturity in relation to people that we both know I did not have. It has made me less quick to judge, more tolerant and understanding. I do not know if this growth would have occurred had I not gone into police work, but I do know that it is a definite and real and very important thing.

There are certain questions that will inevitably come from those who know me and have worked with me, and hopefully from my readers who become acquainted with me for the first time through this book. Are the people real? Did the events described here really happen? Was I personally involved in the events described?

The answer to all these questions (and I am not straining unnecessarily for ambiguity) must be "yes and no." Are the people represented here real? Yes, of course. But there is no person in this book, including the writer, who is portrayed exactly as he appears in real life; each character is based on someone I have come to know or have observed, or on someone I have seen fleetingly who has left an indelible impression for one reason or another. Each person represented merely serves the writer as the means by which the story must be told.

Did these things really happen? All things on earth have really happened. All great things, all terrible things, all mundane things have happened, will happen again, for people do not change, and they make their own events or are carried along by events not of their own making. In that sense, the stories are true, but they are fashioned by the writer's imagination, combined with the acquired knowledge of the policewoman. I feel it is my obligation as a writer to be selective, to change and maneuver facts into an orderly combination, to build and shape and mold for the purposes of dramatic interest and logicality, in such a way as to reveal what the writer has found to be the truth.

Was I personally involved in the events described in this book? In almost every instance, to some degree, I would have to say yes. Now, before a group of my colleagues roll their eyes heavenward, the policewoman must explain—the writer is called upon to give no explanations. To some degree, I say yes, I was involved—as any police officer, active in the field of law enforcement, and encountering *like experiences,* gains an *emotional understanding* of events in which he does not actively participate. The events related in this book are based on things that have happened to me and things that have happened to other police officers. Policemen are the world's greatest storytellers, and my police career has been a remarkable opportunity for a writer to sit and listen as they weave their stories. It was the writer who registered these events; it was the police officer who understood them.

Perhaps this, then, is why the book was written. To show you, outside the world of the police officer, the way it is.

The way it really is.

Dorothy Uhnak
Detective
New York City Transit Police Department.

1

"A strange world, a terrible world, a familiar world"

It might have been the insistently intrusive warm April air that made us restless that morning, or it might have been the droning hum of the lecturer's voice, or it might have been the knowledge that this was the last morning of classes. Though most people have a natural affinity for their birth-month, I have always been uneasy in April, for it is one of those beginning months: I don't like beginnings of things or endings of things. In May, it is definitely spring, the indecision is gone, the shifting between grayness and sunlight, between warmth and mean chill is over, and we are plunged into the steady heat of summer. September is another month I find hard: the remnants of summer cling, the indications of winter are sly and not clear-cut transitions. There is always a restlessness, a kind of wary, eager, nervous anticipation to get to the heart of things during these fringe months: get into the heat and learn to live with it; get into the cold and complain bitterly, but be in it.

Perhaps this was one of the reasons for the agitation. The class of police recruits shifted and scuffled; the young men, dressed in somewhat crumpled gray twill uniforms, were in various stages of motion or sunk in lifeless immobility. My white dress shirt felt starchy and the heavy navy blue uniform skirt was sticky and thick, and the black tie, with its uncomfortable knot, was like a noose.

My attention became focused on the man sitting to my left—or rather on his right hand, which was tapping an infuriating beat: one-two-three, one-two, one-two. He was accompanying his finger dance with a breathy soft whistle. Two seats beyond him, a black shoe was kicking at the

1

air in time to some inner music. One of the men two rows
ahead of me was sprawled out, his legs apparently thrust
forward, judging from the position of his light curly head
resting on the back of his chair; his arms were looped over
the chairs on either side of him. His neighbor to the left,
a slight, nervous type, was leaning forward anxiously to
avoid pressing against the burly arm. The girl to my right
was tracing a flower over and over on her note pad: the
petals were long, delicate, swaying arrows, pointing toward
a round, black, spiky sun. The faces all around me were
like faces in a trance: it was as though everyone in the
room, except me, was hypnotized by the unaccustomed
measure of heat and by the relentless hum of the book-
lieutenant who was speaking about something. What? I
tried to concentrate, to blink away the lazy blending of
sound into a stream of meaninglessness, to catch the individual words. He spoke in a loud and even tone, but he
was completely devoid of vitality. Something about the
law of search and seizure. Search and seizure. I relaxed,
keeping my eyes from blinking, giving up the effort and
letting myself slip into the encompassing coma that covered us all like an inverted cup. It was no effort to move
from the irritating, jangling sounds, from the tappings and
creakings of boredom-heavy bodies unable to adjust to the
inadequate metal chairs, or from the droning instructional
voice. The sounds were a dull, even background for my
own thoughts.

It was somehow odd that the long weeks of lectures
and demonstrations had not deadened me, had not dimin-
ished the sense of intoxication that would suddenly, unexpectedly burst through me at the most unlikely times,
triggered by a word, a phrase. It was an excitement that
could never be revealed to anyone here: not to the other
three girls attending the Police Academy with me in this
class of one hundred and four police recruits. But I would
go home in the evenings and in recounting the day to
Tony would find a sense of reality springing from the
sections of the Penal Code and the Code of Criminal Procedure that we had to memorize and were tested on each
week. They related to people, these words couched in

incomprehensible legal terms, to acts committed by people I was to move among.

And Tony, familiar with my earnest dedication to whatever I threw myself into, would let me talk, would let the thing grow and swell around us. Then I would stop, finally aware that my throat was dry and that I had been speaking for hours and that he had been listening, leading me on with his grave attention, and we would both laugh. "Oh, God," I'd finally say, "you know what? The classes today were as boring as the devil!"

But that wasn't completely true either. Though the air about us had been thick with the hum of ineffectual lecturers, there was still a pervading hint of reality in all of it. As we had walked through the musty room which housed a kind of police museum, looking, in groups of four and five, at exhibits of weapons, narcotics, fragments of evidence which had cracked seemingly insoluble cases of murder and destruction, some element of excitement had managed to break through. For me, at least, each yellowing card pasted on the exhibition boards beneath the glass cases, telling in terse and unimaginative words the step-by-step method of investigation, led to speculation on *the people* involved: those who had done these terrible and incredible things, and those who had discovered and revealed them. I was fascinated by the actual weapons: the gun which had actually shot down four people, been held by some demented man, been wrenched from his grasp by a police officer whose only thoughts at that moment had been on that particular gun in that particular hand. For him, nothing else in the entire world had existed at that particular moment. The cards were inadequate: too coldly written, failing to show the emotion, to show the thing as it must have been. Even these things were somehow made dull and unreal in their presentation.

They showed us movies—those grayish-white documentaries designed to stimulate your resolve to do your job efficiently and with honor. Young, clean-cut, carefully selected policemen showed you how to search a prisoner, how to place his feet so many inches from a wall, his hands resting against the wall in such a manner that you had a kind of safety device against him. If he moved so much as an inch, your foot could swing out quickly in front of his, and he would fall on his face. And then we practiced—or rather, we girls watched the men practice —patting each other down. The women, we were told, were not often called upon to search men, and we would learn from other policewomen the procedures whereby women prisoners were searched.

Then an older policeman, a detective, would appear and challenge the recruits to search him, warning them in advance that he was heavily armed. A bright-eyed rookie would place him just so, run his hands along the detective's arms and shoulders and body and legs, and place a gun or two on the table, maybe a knife. He would stand back, satisfied, and then "die" when the detective casually peeled an automatic revolver, two switchblade knives, a .32 Smith and Wesson, brass knuckles and a jack from his person. It was a demonstration designed partly to shock, but mainly to warn and to instruct, and it made a strong impression on us. Of course, it made an unforgettable impression on the recruit who had diligently searched the "prisoner."

There was physical fitness training, too, but again we girls were excused. We were invited as spectators to the judo sessions, to observe basic karate slashes, but the instructor, a beefy man with a flat face, twisted ears and beady gray eyes, wanted no part of us and cast a watery sneer at our requests to try a toss or a slash or two. We spent those hours with older policewomen, listening to their stories, and wondering. They spoke so casually about it all: about arrests, about the taking of a prisoner into custody. You wondered if it was all really like that, or if they were just enjoying their effect on us.

We all took part in firearms training. The men had standard service revolvers and the prospective policewomen had .32 Smith and Wesson revolvers. My mother paid for my gun. A strange present from a mother to a twenty-one-year-old daughter, I suppose—my first gun. But it was in fulfillment of a promise, long forgotten by me, that my mother had made when I was about ten years old. "When you become a policewoman, I'll buy your gun for you." We were both unsettled to learn that a gun cost fifty-four dollars—and this at a special rate. The expenditure for my uniforms was another jolt; it cost close to two hundred and fifty dollars to buy the required skirt, jacket, overcoat (that was so heavy you could hardly hold your shoulders up), hat (that wouldn't stay on your head), sling-pocketbook (that allowed for revolver and notebook and counted on your not needing lipstick, comb or even a handkerchief). The shoes were medium-height black pumps. "Make sure they're comfortable, you'll be standing on them quite a bit." The white shirts were regulation, which meant uniformly uncomfortable, and the black tie and clasp were foreign to us; fathers or husbands or brothers stood patiently each morning, arms looped over shoulders, watching in the mirror, trying to teach us how to make the incredible, stupid knot.

I had seen guns before, of course: in the holsters of policemen, in the hands of swift cowboys and movie desperados. But having a gun of your own, holding it in your hand, loading it with bullets and being responsible for it, is another matter altogether. The shooting range was located in the center of Central Park, in a building adjoining the park precinct. Here there was no discrimination: man or woman, you had a gun and you had to learn to handle it. They showed us charts which described the way your sights should look when you held the gun at arm's length and fired at the target. Three even little ridges should stick up at a level; there should be a tiny, exactly equal space on each side of the middle ridge, and the center ridge should be lined up with the center of the bull's-eye. When I shot my gun for the first time, I was somewhat prepared for the blast; it was an ear-shattering, resounding blast, echoing down the long chamber of the shooting range, with a simultaneous flash of fire. But the feeling of the gun in my hand was unexpected: the jump, or thrust. My hand, outstretched, was trembling; the gun seemed to get heavier and heavier as I tried to hold the revolver in the way shown on the chart. An instructor stood behind my right shoulder, telling me to rest my arm on the counter in front of me. As I started to turn toward him, he held my right arm tightly. You should never turn your gun-hand around; you keep it facing down the alley. Firearms instructors are the bravest men I have ever known.

I had thought I would take to shooting easily; this, too, was to be a natural thing for me. But there is nothing natural about shooting a gun, and I stared in disbelief at my target when I reeled it in with the little handle that sends it waving up and down the alley. I had fired ten bullets but there were only two holes in the target—just two, and those were on the outside rim. The instructor explained with infinite patience that you do not *pull* the trigger. "You squeeze, you squeeze, you squeeze," he intoned softly, "until it becomes inevitable, automatic, a natural conclusion and an extension of your arm, your hand, your finger." Squeeze—the magic word. I practiced at home for hours holding a milk bottle at arm's length, to steady my arm, to rid myself of the quiver; I practiced "dry-shooting," with the six bullets in sight on my dresser, pointing the emptied gun toward some imaginary spot, dead center on the target. Cock with your thumb and squeeze, squeeze. Throughout a police career, we learned, there are periodic practice sessions, and if you don't achieve a qualifying score on the allotted bullets, you start purchasing bullets. I could see that this shooting business was going to be a continuing expense.

We were taken on tours of the courts, a bewildering network of buildings: General Sessions, Special Sessions, Felony Court, Magistrate's Court, Gambler's Court, Women's Court, Youth Term. Here you write up the complaint, after putting your prisoner in the custody of the Department of Correction officers. If it's a felony, of course, you present him at the photo gallery in the basement of police headquarters for some picture-taking. And you arrive with his rap sheet, his yellow sheet, his criminal record which you have obtained from the Bureau of Criminal Identification. The Bureau has obtained said rap sheet through a search based on your prisoner's pedigree sheet, which you had filled out at the precinct (when his fingerprints were taken) prior to booking. Then you escort your prisoner to the appropriate jurisdiction and follow your case through to its completion, the satisfactory completion being a conviction. This is when we all became silent and when the wisecracks stopped—at the realization of the total responsibility that would be placed on each of us.

Oh, God, he was still talking, that poor lieutenant, completely unaware of, or maybe accustomed to, the fact that he had long since lost his audience. These were the initiation rites, I thought, the hated beginnings that had to be gotten through. When these were over and done with, I could put them from my mind, these hours, because no word spoken here in this hazy, grayish room had any relation to the world out there that we were soon to enter. It flashed through me again, that persistent, recurring feeling, like a chill: I'm really here, I'm really getting into it. I looked around at all of them, completely aware now of myself and where I was, but feeling like a twelve-year-old who has sneaked in disguised, and gotten away with it.

There was a silence in the room now, and it filled the air with a kind of lightness, it was so unexpected. Apparently, the lecture was over, for the lieutenant was gathering up his pencils, closing his folder of papers. Everyone in the room was moving slowly, purposelessly, stretching, muttering the usual bitterly funny comments about this lieutenant's ability to murder us all with words. What charge do you give him? Verbal strangulation in the third?

Mary Leary, the girl to my right, asked if my husband would be at the ceremonies tomorrow, and what time we were supposed to be there, anyway? The noise of the voices and moving chairs became louder, the sighs and relieved groans mingled with questions and answers and greetings hooted across the room. Some of the men were struggling along the uneven rows of chairs, scraping them out of line to get into the aisles.

A voice cut through the room like a scythe. "Attention!"

We all froze in place, not glancing at each other, but looking up to the lecture platform and the straight navy blue figure of a captain we hadn't seen before. He did not call out a second time, but stood, unmoving, dead-center, glaring coldly down at us until there wasn't a sound anywhere and until each recruit present somewhat self-consciously drew his feet together, put his shoulders back slightly and let his hands fall more or less stiffly at his sides. The captain stood motionless as the room slowly molded itself into straight lines of gray-clad men, one behind the other, each in front of a metal bridge chair, with four girls standing in front of chairs at the right side of the room. The captain's eyes swept the room, stopping at a particular section, and that section turned slowly to steel, rigidly perfect. For a full minute, there was not even the sound of breathing. And then he spoke again.

"Deputy Inspector George J. Harrington will now address this assembly."

He turned smartly in his shiny black shoes and faced to his right, saluted briskly as the tall, gray-haired man approached and returned his salute. The deputy inspector surveyed us, and at some hidden signal, which somehow communicated itself to everyone in the room, we all saluted. The D.I. returned the salute and told us to be seated.

He was a tall man with a bitter face and a very low voice, which he did not trouble to raise. Yet he could be heard in the very last row, and it was obvious that he intended to hold the attention of every person in that room.

"Tomorrow, you will all graduate from the Police Academy and you will all become probationary members of the Police Department of the City of New York."

His tone was not commendatory; there was something almost scornful in his voice. If we had expected a routine speech of congratulations and welcome, we knew immediately that this was not to be it.

"I don't know any of you; not by name, or sight or reputation. I don't know your capabilities or your possibilities. I don't know if there is, in this room, one person who will become a good police officer or one person who will become a bad police officer. I do know that you have had the benefit of the finest academic training the Police Department can offer you. How much or how little you have benefited from this instruction is not measured by the examination marks you have achieved during the last three months. Don't congratulate yourselves if you have done well on these little examinations: it is no measure of what kind of cop you're going to be."

One rookie patrolman in the third row blushed furiously. He had finished number-one man and was to be presented with an award the next day.

"I don't know what brought any of you here, why you want to be police officers. I don't know if your reasons are good ones or bad ones, or what you expect to get from the job, or what you are bringing to it."

The inspector's tone and manner clearly indicated we were all suspect: our motivations and capabilities were all clear to him. He knew.

"But I do know about policemen and the world of policemen. I've been in that world for twenty-three years. There is little you can gain by what I've experienced —you are going to have to live it yourself. But I will tell you what it is to be a police officer, and you can start out with this, and think about it and turn it over in your own mind, and don't say you weren't warned."

There was a slight sound in the room; the D.I. stopped speaking, and a cough was stifled and a sneeze swallowed and an exchange of glances halted in mid-air before he would continue.

"This is your city, and most of you have lived here all your lives. But you don't know this city and you don't know its people. I don't care what backgrounds you come from or what neighborhoods you were raised in. You don't know it because you haven't seen it, but you are going to see it now with policeman's eyes, and I advise you to put aside any illusions you might have. There is dirt and corruption and moral disease and agony and tragedy, and you are going to be a part of it."

His voice was as soft as before; it just seemed louder—

or clearer, perhaps—because of the words. They were sharp and familiar to me; I had heard them before, somewhere. They were known to me, somehow.

"I don't mean the stories you read in the newspapers or the pictures of a murder victim's wife and children or a dope addict's cravings, as detailed in syndicated articles by sob sisters. No matter how graphically described, these stories skim the surface, and you as police officers are going to go down into the depths. You are going to touch and handle and encounter the living flesh and the dying blood."

There was no theatrical quality to his words. He spoke them too calmly, too matter-of-factly.

"Your whole lives are going to change, and the people closest to you are going to be the first ones to suffer from it. You will deal with the vilest and the lowest and the most depraved forms of humanity, and if you think you can walk away from it lily-pure, turn in your shields right now. Because it will touch you and rub off on you and become a part of you, and what shocks you now will become merely routine to you within a very short time. You will learn not to feel another person's tears; you will learn that you are not your brother's keeper; you will learn that another man's troubles are not yours. You had better learn this, and the sooner the better."

The deputy inspector glared at us, his jaw jutting out. He was like some minister preaching a new and almost profane doctrine and defying anyone to cross him, to deny him. We sat staring back at him, a strong cord of fascination uniting us with him.

"When you start working out in the field," he said, encompassing us all with his quiet, rational voice, "you will find yourself judging the older, more experienced police officer. You will look at him and see that he is unmoved by what is happening around him; that he can examine a butchered or headless piece of a corpse with something like curiosity, and go to his meal an hour later and eat an egg sandwich and drink coffee and laugh and joke, and you will think he is some kind of monster. But you had better go along with him and eat your sandwich and drink your coffee and laugh and joke, and the sooner the better. You had better learn to develop that shell around you. We didn't teach you about a shell here at the Academy, did we? Well, you have to learn that one for yourself. Develop a rotten, stinking shell, a hard, impenetrable shell against all emotions and all feelings. Your wife will notice it first, and your kids. I could tell you to leave it at the station house or in the squad room, but you won't. You can't, because you're not going to be working with papers and numbers and words and figures. You're going to be working with human beings, and you will see them at their worst and in their most terrible moments, and if you relax and let that wall around you crack for a moment, it will get hold of you and eat your guts out. Your wife will worry about you and learn to hate your job. There isn't a policeman's wife anywhere who likes her husband's job or what it does to him. Your kids will find out that having a father who's a cop is not like in the movies or the television stories. You will be quicker to jump on them, quicker to look for the warning signs in them, because you've seen what another man's child has done. You will see what men are capable of doing, and I will tell you this: men are capable of every crime in the book."

His words were addressed to the men, but he had seen us, the policewomen, sitting there in the first row before him. He had seen us in one hard, scornful, open glance, and then had dismissed us. If he had his serious doubts and suspicions of the men before him, there was no question of his feelings toward the women present.

His voice was not monotonous, but it was the words rather than his delivery of them that gave him a kind of blazing life. It was almost as though he were struggling to suppress some strong and urgent emotion which must be controlled with a soft voice, must not be allowed to slip from his lips in an unguarded moment.

"Every man is capable of every crime, and there is no horrible, unimaginable crime. Every one of them has been committed in the past, and will be committed in the future. Think of that for a moment." And he actually stopped speaking, and we actually thought about it for a moment, such was his command in that room.

"Now," he said, ending our train of thought which he had set in motion, "you are going to find out that the only brother you have in the world is your brother police officer; he is the only man in the world you can talk to who will understand you. Not your blood brother, whom you were raised with and lived with all your growing years. If he isn't a cop too, you and he will be speaking about the same things to each other in different languages. You will have more in common with a village constable in a town of four hundred people than you will with your own brother because that village constable lives in the same world as the first-grade detective in any city in the world; he has seen people with the same eyes, the cop's eyes. Most people are aware of the insularity of a police group; they give various interpretations to this insularity, mostly of a derogatory nature. But you will find, as you become police officers, that this is not only a natural development, but an essential one, because only a policeman, a working policeman, can understand the policeman's language and the policeman's world and the policeman's life. It is foreign and incomprehensible to everyone else and it cannot be communicated to them."

The deputy inspector did not speak from any papers or cards; he spoke from some deep place within himself, almost from some great need to tell us these things, to communicate them to us, to let us know. That his manner and tone were far from ingratiating did not seem to matter; his rapport with us was complete. His tone never varied, except perhaps that it became softer; we leaned forward, listening harder.

"You will gradually come to think in terms of two worlds, theirs (the general public's) and ours, and you will come to recognize and accept the bitter fact that the average law-abiding citizen views us with a certain distaste. He feels it is his constitutional right to abuse us verbally. But you, on the other hand, must not return that hostility. We set you up, in your blue uniform, as a target for every crackpot and nut around. You are identified, you are a public servant, and the public expects service from those on its payroll. Accept this as part of the price you must pay for the job you do. Accept it and the fact that you are alone when you are working and the only guy who will stick his neck out for you is another cop. Don't expect anything else from anyone else—it will not be forthcoming.

"I am not going to tell you what your job is; you've had three months of the finest instruction of its kind in the world. But I will tell you that your job is *not to judge* either your fellow officer or the people you will arrest. Your major concern at this point in your career will be to adjust to the world you are about to enter. It is a definite, distinct, strange, terrible world, a familiar world, distorted out of all probability. Little by little, you will learn to focus on things that were invisible to you before. In years to come, you will look back on the time before you were a police officer and wonder how you could have existed in this very same city without seeing all the things you will have learned to see and to know."

The deputy inspector had dismissed my presence, but he was speaking directly to me; his words were formed and shaped and spoken to me, accepted by me, understood by me. It was as though, finally, finally, through all these weeks and days and hours of touching lightly on the fringes, finally, someone had stood up and spoken out, honestly, truly, told us. The deputy inspector hunched over the lectern; his voice for the first time seemed to grow weary. He cleared his throat, started out a little louder, then lowered his voice.

"Tomorrow you will have a graduation day and the police commissioner and the mayor will come here and congratulate you and give out the various awards, and your families will be proud of you in your new navy blue uniforms with your shields shining as bright as they will ever be, and you will take pictures of each other.

"And then, from your first tour on, you will begin, *just begin,* to learn what it is to be a policeman. Don't think you know anything at all about it now. You've read the assignments and memorized the laws and procedures and rules and regulations and seen the exhibits and motion pictures and demonstrations and heard the lectures. You will find they translate very differently when put into action.

"I don't know how many of you here present today will continue on this job, or will advance through the ranks, take the tests, get the promotions, but get one thing straight, whatever your aims or goals may be: this is not a job, it is a whole way of life, and if you decide to live it, you will have to live it twenty-four hours a day for as long as you are a police officer!"

And then, Deputy Inspector George J. Harrington was done with us. With a cold look over the room, and one glimpse of unmistakable contempt in our direction—a look which must have caught poor Mary Leary right in the eyes, for she shuddered—he marched off the platform and exited through some door from whence he had come.

There was an almost stunned silence in the room, a kind of unwillingness to begin, and even after the captain with the loud voice dismissed us, most of us just sat quietly, thinking or absorbing the words that had surrounded us like so many soft, quiet threats.

"Jesus Christ," a voice from the middle of the room rang out, "what a real sweet man that was!"

There was a burst of relieved laughter, for this, now, could be handled, put in its proper place, laughed about. The remarks began flowing now, but underneath the crisp, fast, bright humor there was a certain, definite uneasiness. He had put it on the line, he had told us the way it was, and that could not be laughed or cursed or joked away. He had the look of a man who knew, and he had, for some reasons of his own, tried to tell us.

2

"Start to know it; start to live it"

I will say this about the Police Department: they don't
fool around. You finish the training they allot to you and
then you get down to work. You are placed where you are
needed, and if you don't feel adequately prepared for
the assignment given, you prepare yourself adequately on
the job.

At the Academy, the 8 A.M. to 4 P.M. workday and the
Monday through Friday work week were taken for
granted. My first assignment was matron duty, midnight
tour: you arrive on the job at 11:30 P.M., relieving the
policewoman on the 4 to midnight shift a half-hour early,
a traditional courtesy from which you benefit at 7:30 the
next morning when the next girl comes on duty. The
adjustments you have to make in your living arrangements are solely your concern. If you find it difficult to
go to bed when you arrive home at 8:30 in the morning, that is a shame, but there you are. If you do manage
to get to sleep and miraculously sleep until 3 or 4 in
the afternoon, you begin to wonder what meal you are
supposed to be eating, and then settle for a cup of tea
to hold you until suppertime. I ate supper with Tony
when he came home at 6 o'clock. I showered at 8 and
prepared for my evening as he relaxed for his. He went
to bed at 10:30 as I left for work, carrying a sandwich
in my pocketbook, wondering what ever happened to
breakfast.

The duty chart had been explained to us and re-ex-
plained to us, but it still didn't make much sense. It was
impossible to figure how many actual days you worked
when a day began at 12 midnight (wasn't that "tomor-

row"?) and ended when most people were beginning their workday. All I really knew was that Saturdays and Sundays were out, so forget about them. Sooner or later, as I advanced along the duty chart, I would find that I had week ends off—maybe even around Christmas, which would be nice, in a way.

The precinct in Harlem to which I was assigned had only one resemblance to the 46th Precinct of my childhood: there were two green lanterns flanking the entrance. For the rest, it fitted in perfectly with its neighboring buildings: it was ancient, gray, musty, in dangerous repair, ugly, depressing and uncomfortable.

My office, a dreary cubicle on the second floor, up an iron staircase screened with mesh, was fitted out with a battered couch—the kind psychiatrists use when relaxing people into a talking fit, a "captain's chair," scarred and yellow with chipping shellac, two nondescript wooden chairs, one regulation gray desk with a blackish rubber-like top and one small electric hot plate with a pot for boiling water. The policewoman whom I was relieving had sleep lines creased deep along her cheeks and the corners of her eyes, which she rubbed briskly. She stretched and then told me that the "guests" were sleeping; there were three women prisoners being detained for the night. I shouldn't anticipate any problems with them: two were drunks and one was a prostitute—nothing very important. She indicated the couch, opened the bottom desk drawer and pulled out some ragged paperback books and told me to take life easy.

Sitting alone in the room now, feeling the silence of the place, I didn't know what I was supposed to do. I had made the entry in my memorandum book: on duty such and such a place, such and such a time, et cetera. And now, here I was: on duty. I fluttered through the pocket books. All stories about private detectives and beautiful but criminally inclined blondes or red-haired creatures of fantastic physical attainments. I decided to take a look at my charges, but worried that they might hear me and wake up. Finally, walking softly, feeling somehow an intruder, I unlocked the outer door and glanced in at the row of detention cells, counted three sleeping forms in the cells, then closed the door. I boiled a pot of water, then found there was only instant coffee, and made a mental note to bring in some tea bags. I looked out the window through the wiremesh guard, but the building faced on a brick wall. I walked to the doorway. The hall was deserted and soundless. There was a familiar smell in the building, reminiscent of all public buildings—a smell of people and shoes and old cigarettes and stale cigars and clothing and time. I walked quietly, feeling a vague sense of guilty invasion, toward the Detective Squad Room. There was a light on, a small fluorescent lamp glowing bluely on the surface of an empty desk; there was a hat on the rack and a small light shining from the inner office. I entered the room far enough to see a pair of feet on a cot in the inner office; then I turned and exited to the hall, nearly colliding with a big man, a Negro, whose hat was set back off his forehead. I caught my breath in a kind of embarrassment, intimidated by his face. He was regarding me without surprise, but with a certain narrowing of his dark, glinting eyes.

"Looking for something?"

"Yes," I said, "the . . . er, the ladies room."

He lifted one of the paper bags he was holding, clutched in a large hand the way a child holds a parcel. "We all use that one." He indicated a room down the hall. "Just close the door and it's a ladies room."

"I'm on duty here, I'm on matron duty," I said, feeling some explanation, some excuse for my presence was indicated.

"Yeah," he said with a warm, rich amusement not touching his eyes, just playing around his mouth. My uniform, new, spotless, testified for me. "You want some coffee? We've got an extra container."

I shook my head and he went into the Detective Squad Room. That was all that happened my first night. I sat, I walked around, I read a few pages of each of the pocket books, I tried not to fall asleep, and then, finally, finally, it was morning and another policewoman relieved me. I had never even seen the faces of my prisoners.

I arrived for my second tour, a Friday night—a Saturday morning, really, one minute after midnight changes the day—armed with a novel I'd been meaning to read for a long time, a box of tea bags and an extra pack of cigarettes. I had spotted a manicure set in the bottom drawer and intended to do a little grooming. The second floor was alive with sound: there were heavy male voices from the Detectives' room, typing sounds, moving-around sounds. The policewoman on duty was battering away on an old typewriter, and she ground a cigarette into a loaded ash tray.

"Boy, what a madhouse! Can you type?"

I said that I could, and she stood up, pushing the chair away from the desk. "Boy, they expect you to be a secretary. I'm a hunt-and-find-and-hope-for-the-best kind of typist myself." She looked like a hunt-and-find-and-hope-for-the-best type: her make-up curled up her lips unevenly, her hair was slightly lopsided and the little dabs of eyeliner were haphazard. She flexed her fingers, then rubbed them with quick, annoyed motions. "Listen, I'm typing up a report for Detective Harris. I just started, so maybe you'd take over, if you can read his handwriting. Also, if you can interpret. If this is English, then I'm Dutch, and my name is O'Leary, and I'm not Dutch."

"What's all the commotion?" I asked, trying to be casual, but looking toward the door.

Policewoman O'Leary bent heavily over her shoes, made some adjustment, then grunted as she sat upright. "Oh, just a Friday night in Harlem. You'll get used to it. They got some kids in there—a knifing. Gang stuff, you know. Oh, and there's some girls in there, but the J.A.B.'ll probably send someone around, they look pretty young."

About twenty minutes after she left, I was squinting over the remarkable wordings of Detective LeRoy Harris, wondering just how far I should go in my translation. There was no one in the detention cells, and the noises from down the hall were getting louder, though they were still incomprehensible. Detective Harris' story was anything but vivid. "On information" they had picked up five boys, ages 17 to 20, on suspicion of knifing one Maceo

Littlejohn Johnson, Jr., who was now confined to Harlem Hospital with seven knife wounds inflicted by person(s) unknown at approximately 8:30 P.M. on the corner of Lenox Avenue and 118th Street. The suspects were members of the Black Kings. Three girls, ages 16 to 18, were also picked up on suspicion. I was wondering what the author looked like when he appeared in the doorway. He resembled his handwriting: small, cramped, secretive. His voice was hollow, but at the same time had a harshness. He looked and sounded like a bookie.

"Oh, hey," he said, without any preliminaries, "you got that ready yet? The lieutenant is chewing my head off in there."

He didn't seem to notice that I was not Policewoman O'Leary. "Just about ready. Are you Detective Harris?"

He took the paper from my hand, nodded absently, then stopped at the door. "Oh, hey, thanks," he whispered, without looking at me.

And then I was left alone again, and an hour went by and the noise became louder. I felt very restless and resentful. It was all happening down the hall and somehow I felt I should know what was going on. At least someone should say something to me: I was a policewoman.

A tall, young, dark-haired man, dressed neatly in charcoal gray, white shirt and dark tie, stood in the doorway. "Excuse me, officer, I'm Lieutenant Bouvreau, squad commander of the precinct's detectives."

"Yes, sir. I'm Policewoman Uhnak." I started to rise but he waved me back with a friendly gesture.

"Yes, the desk sergeant told me your name. Dorothy, isn't it?" His voice was soft and polite and friendly, and I warmed at the recognition that was invoked by his use of my first name—finally an acceptance of the fact that I was there. "We have a bit of a problem here." Lieutenant Bouvreau pulled up a rickety chair and straddled it backward, his long hands dangling over the ribs of the chair. Quietly and in some detail he explained that they had three girls in custody and that he felt sure one of the girls would break and tell which of the boys did the actual knifing. Louise Wilcox, he told me, was seventeen years old and they didn't know much about her, except that she didn't seem to be a regular "gang girl." She seemed too timid, too scared by what was going on. He wanted me to talk to her. He looked at me earnestly, ran a long-fingered hand over a boyish cowlick that stood stiffly on his neatly cropped black head, then nodded. "I think you'd do just fine; you're young, not much older than those girls in there. I think Louise is going to need a little sympathy pretty soon." Then he hesitated, the corners of his eyes crinkled. "This is your first assignment, isn't it?"

"Yes, sir." I felt a certain relief in his knowing my circumstance; his silent nodding indicated his awareness of my feelings—an understanding of my resolve to do a good job.

"Well," he said pleasantly, "I want you to come inside with me. Now, you're going to have to play this by ear, Dorothy." Again, the friendly earnestness, but his voice was softer now, and his words were a kind of plea. "Whatever you see or hear in our office is necessary. It's like a game, almost. We have the good guys and the bad guys. The loudmouths are the bad guys; you're going to be a good guy. Get the picture? Louise is going to need a shoulder. We're going to scare the devil out of her. Then she'll want to talk to someone who is sympathetic. Do you feel sympathetic?"

I felt nervous. "I guess I could be."

"I'm sure you will be." His confidence seemed old and familiar, as though based on years of expectation fulfilled.

For the first time, I entered the Detective Squad Room on official business. There were five surly Negro youths standing against one side of the room, and three equally surly Negro detectives aligned in front of them, growling various things at them individually and collectively. One angry young Irish detective was smashing the keys of a reluctant typewriter, muttering at the letters that were appearing on his paper. Detective Harris was whispering into a telephone, his hand cupped around his mouth, his eyes furtive.

In the inner room, the cot was nowhere in evidence, and

three young Negro girls were standing together by the window, staring through the grating. They turned and viewed me blankly.

"This is Policewoman Uhnak," Lieutenant Bouvreau said politely. None of us acknowledged the introduction. The lieutenant indicated two chairs and left. A moment later, one of the detectives brought in two more chairs, then slammed the door behind him.

"I think you'd better sit down," I said, keeping my voice low to control my uncertainty. The three girls didn't move, so I stood up and picked up the pad and pencil that were on the desk against the wall. These were kids. In my settlement house days, some of my best friends were kids. These were no different. I turned and faced them.

"You," I said pleasantly, matter-of-factly, but certain that I meant what I said, "sit here." The girl stood motionless, taking my measure, reading my face and my voice. "Now."

Languidly and with a kind of dignity, she slid herself forward, twisting her mouth into a grimace of annoyed amusement. She'd go along with the gag. But she did sit down, and the two others, watching her, followed her lead.

"No," I said to the second girl, "not there. I want you over here." We watched each other wordlessly, and the tall, thin girl glanced at the first girl, then changed her seat.

I could have picked Louise Wilcox out without help. She was light-skinned, almost yellow; her face was drawn and tired and her fear was shining from her large eyes. She was an unattractive girl, of medium height, flat-chested and shapeless in a mottled pink sweater and stained brown skirt. Her hair was pulled behind her ears in daggers of unruly kinks, and her bangs stood out from her forehead stiffly.

The first girl, obviously the leader here, was pretty and she knew it full well. Her hair was teased high and perched on her head like a tumbleweed, perfectly round. It looked like it would blow away with any sudden gust of wind. Her face was skillfully made up, her eyes bright and black as Chinese checkers. She wore a tight red skirt and sweater, and her figure was slender and graceful.

"Whut for they grab us in here and push us aroun'? We didn't do nuthin'."

Her speech, I felt, was something of an affectation. She had an intelligent face; she was playing a game.

"Well, I guess you know why. Those boys in there—they're your friends?"

"Friends? Ha, hear that police-lady?" She pointed at me and the girl next to her grinned. "Friends? Man, them cats in there, they don't call their chicks friends!"

She laughed uproariously, but without humor, without any sounds of joy, and her eyes watched me closely. It was meant to be an insulting sound, and the other girl joined in, cued and careful. Louise's hands trembled and she was silent. Her fingers were bony and yellow. She kept her head down.

The door opened so unexpectedly that I dropped my pencil. It was the Negro detective I had seen the night before in the hallway. He glared in meanly, his eyes darting over the girls. "Which one of these is Louise?" His voice was low and menacing.

Louise looked up, panic twitching her mouth. He looked at her, then nodded his head up and down, pulled at his mouth. "Yeah," he said. "Yeah." He stood for a fraction of a moment, then left, slamming the door.

We sat silently now; Louise was at the edge of her chair, the toes of the scuffed shoes digging into the floor.

"Hey," the first girl said, poking her sharply, "that's just their tricks. Like they tryin' to scare you is all."

"I think you'd better shut up," I said pleasantly to girl number one, and she drew her head up, pushing her pointed chin at me and making a small clicking sound with her tongue against her teeth.

Lieutenant Bouvreau's calm face appeared at the doorway. "Miss, I want you to come with me, and you too, please," he said, nodding at the two girls. Louise started to rise, but the lieutenant shook his head at her. "You're Louise, right? No, you stay here." There was no hint, no message in his voice.

Louise stared at him, her mouth slack and her teeth shining.

Girl number one swayed herself to the door, thrusting her hips out before her, then turned. Her eyes blazed and her voice was a hiss. "Hey, you Louise-girl, keep your fat mouth shut!" Some dark hand pulled her quickly through the door, and we could hear her insulted voice calling out curses. There was a great deal of clamor and banging and shouting.

Louise gaped at me; the skin around her mouth seemed to tighten and pale. Her face was yellowish-gray now, pulled by fear.

"How come," she asked softly, "how come they keep looking in an' sayin' 'Louise' at me? I didn't do nuthin'. How come?"

Her voice was thin and it broke on her words. I couldn't look at her. "Louise, how old are you?" We went through a long list of questions: anything I could think of to keep from seeing her face. I knew she kept watching the door, trying to steel herself to the sudden opening, the peering hostile faces looking at her, saying her name. The use of your first name, I thought, could evoke many feelings.

The door swung open again. This time the Irish detective pushed his way in. He had a middle-aged Negro by the arm, a small, roundish man with horn-rimmed glasses on his smooth face. He propelled the man into the room and placed him directly in front of Louise's chair. Then he twisted the neck of the small lamp on the desk so that it shone on the girl's face, paling her features. Her eyes sparkled with terror.

"Now," the detective said, "you take a real good, slow, careful look, Mr. Morris. This is probably going to be a homicide case, and we don't want any mistakes." And then, very carefully, his words ringing like a bell, "Is this the girl?"

Louise seemed to turn to clay as the man studied her, circled her, came and stood in front of her. He took off his glasses, held them against his round body, then put them on again.

"Yes," he said firmly. "No question about it. It's her."

And then they left without another word. Louise leaned forward to me as I continued to write words on the paper. She tapped her hand compulsively on the desk. Her voice was a sick sound. "Hey, how come they keep on doin' that? How come they keep lookin' at me? I don't know that man, I never seen that man. Hey, what they doin' here?"

I handed the girl a cigarette, and my hand trembled when I lit hers and then my own. Her panic was infectious and I felt somehow intimidated, accused by the opening door, the knowing faces. "How long have you been hanging around with that crowd, Louise?"

Her shoulders jerked. "They just 'the kids.' You know. They just live on the block."

"Do you like them?" I asked. She shrugged, inhaling and blowing smoke into her eyes. I realized that she wasn't a smoker, but she seemed unaware of what she was doing. "You know, it seems strange to me; you don't seem like those other girls. You know, they're pretty tough—that's what they think, anyway. You don't seem like that kind of girl, the kind of girl to get into trouble like this."

"But I didn't do nuthin'. I'm not a bad girl, never got no police trouble."

"Well, you've got it now, big trouble," I said cruelly, ignoring my own voice, my own words. "You know what I think, Louise? I think those 'friends' of yours in there are setting you up."

She jerked her face up; her lips were dry and her left eye had started to twitch.

"I mean it. You don't know what they're saying in there. I don't think they'd try to put it on those other two girls: I think they're putting it all on you."

The possibility of it encompassed her. She was fully aware of her status with the "kids"; she was the logical one to put something on, the one who didn't matter. I was being a "friend" to Louise. Talk to me, Louise, you can trust me.

There was an explosion of sound and action in the next room, and we both looked toward the door. Heavy mas-

culine voices were shouting, booming. There was a scuffling, tussling, grunting sound, but then it was subdued.
The girl stared at me.

"You know what, Louise? I don't think they're worth
your little finger. You go to school—you said you'd like
to be a nurse someday. What are they going to be, those
other two girls? Not much more than what they are right
now. You'd better take care of number one, Louise—that's
what they're doing in there. How come they left you
here, how come they keep looking in at you, and asking
for Louise?" The next time the door opened, I thought it
was going to come off at the hinges. A distraught woman,
held back by two detectives, came shrieking into the
room, sailing right at the girl. I jumped up and stood
between them, but someone pushed me aside. Louise
cringed back in her chair and the woman, a heavy-set
Negro woman with an impassioned face, lunged for her,
but was restrained.

"That the bitch kill my boy? That the bitch?" the woman howled. And then they dragged her out and there was
a terrible silence in the room. Louise was gray. Her hands
were pale and shaking violently, and she didn't move from
the chair. Her feet were drawn tightly around the legs,
her body hunched forward, her eyes rolling wildly.

Lieutenant Bouvreau entered the room, stepped inside
and closed the door behind him. He regarded Louise, a
sad expression on his handsome, even features; he shook
his head.

"That was Maceo's mother. He died fifteen minutes
ago. Listen, Louise," he spoke gently, squatting beside her
chair, "I don't think it was murder, I really don't." The
girl regarded him with popping eyes, and there were small
bubbles of saliva in the corners of her mouth. "I think he
did something to you. Something bad. Did he hurt you?"
He spoke as gently as one does to an injured child, assur-
ing his sympathy, his understanding. "Did Maceo do something bad to make you stab him?"

Louise made gulping sounds in her throat but no words
reached her mouth.

"Hey, look," he said, "I think maybe you'd rather talk

to Policewoman Uhnak. You can tell her what Maceo did, you don't have to be ashamed. I'm on your side. If he did what I think he did, you have nothing to worry about. I've heard a lot of bad things about Maceo." Lieutenant Bouvreau stood up, put his hand on the girl's shoulder. "You tell Mrs. Uhnak here all about it." He winked solemnly at her, then left us alone.

Louise began to sob now, convulsively, in great dry, gasping breaths. "They puttin' it on me. I'm scared. Oh, lady, I'm scared they kill me."

I tried not to see her face, but the clutching, wringing spasms of her hands were even worse. "I don't believe it, Louise. I think they're putting it on you because they don't care a thing about you. Listen, Louise, I believe you. I can see what kind of a girl you are, but they're going to stick together unless we can prove it was different. Don't you worry about them. They're not worrying about you. Tell me what really happened. I believe you."

I was telling the girl: You are nothing—not a thing in the eyes of the people most important in your narrow little world. You are nothing. That's exactly what I was saying.

Louise looked up in one great effort, in one tormented resolve. "It were Frenchy. He cut Maceo 'cause Maceo was foolin' with his girl, that little snip Marci in there, and Maceo told Frenchy he could take any ole bitch he felt like and he could take Marci if he felt like it, and they started to fight like that. Marci give Frenchy the knife, and we wuz all there. I seen it, but I swear to God I didn't have nuthin' to do with it." And then, in some remote puzzlement, her face blank, "Nobody would fight over me. She had the knife, Marci, and then Frenchy give her the knife again and she put it in her bra and we all run in different ways, up and down the street, and I got picked up about an hour later in my house, and the cops brung us all here. But I swear to God, they kill me, they know I talk about it. They said, they said." And there was no question but that Louise believed it, for she sobbed uncontrollably into the handkerchief I had given her, a tearless, strangulating sound.

In less than an hour, after being confronted with a first-degree murder charge, Marci revealed where she had hidden the knife. By then, Frenchy was boasting openly that he had killed his enemy and proved his manhood, and was asking if the reporters were going to take his picture for the newspapers.

But the victim hadn't died; it had all been part of the plan. When questioned at the hospital, swathed in bandages, blood feeding into him through tubes, he sneered at the idea of mentioning his assailant's name. It was the code; he would plan his own street vengeance when his hero's wounds had healed.

By three o'clock in the morning, the office had emptied out. The girls had been taken to Girls' Youth House by officers from the J.A.B. unit and the boys, according to their ages, were similarly detained. I helped the men type their reports: statements taken from the boys and from the other two girls. Long, rambling, almost irrational accounts of the same event viewed from different eyes: a heroic event, a matter-of-fact event, a justified event, a Friday-night event. I was a great success in the Squad room because of my fast touch-typing. They got me a container of tea, and I drank it even though the luncheonette man had loaded it with sugar.

My own office seemed even emptier now: the gray walls had a greenish cast. My eyes were tired and smarting. My throat hurt from smoking too many cigarettes, and my mouth tasted stale and dirty. Lieutenant Bouvreau came in and smiled.

"You did a nice job in there, Dorothy. I want to thank you."

I was too tired for feelings, yet there was a feeling there behind the weariness. "What will happen to Louise?"

"Nothing," he said. Then watching me closely, he added, "It was a nasty thing, wasn't it? But then, stabbing a boy on the street seven times is a nasty thing, too."

"And Louise doesn't count?" I hadn't meant to sound angry, but I was too exhausted to regulate my emotions.

"No," he said evenly, "not really. That sounds awful to you, doesn't it? But it's true. Louise just doesn't count."

He stood up then. "Why don't you stretch out for a while. It'll be quiet for the rest of the tour."

I shook my head.

"Aren't you tired?" he asked. "How do you feel?"

His eyes were bright, studying me in a curious, interested way.

"Dirty," I said. "I feel so dirty that I don't think I'll ever scrub the dirt off me, that's how I feel!"

Lieutenant Bouvreau smiled without amusement, and his voice was tinged with just a trace, just a hint of annoyance. "Oh, it'll scrub off. Just don't scrub too hard and rub the skin off, too. You'll need it. Tomorrow it'll be Saturday night. This was just a warm-up."

On Saturday night-Sunday morning, the squad made a big narcotics pinch. I heard the feet thumping up the stairs at about 1:30 A.M. and I put aside the Sunday papers. There was loud talking. It was a moment before I realized that it was Spanish. Detective Tyewells, the Negro with his hat forever clinging to the back of his head, ducked in.

"Hey, Uhnak," he said in his musical voice, "we've got a woman in here. Want a complete search and right now."

I left my charges, two prostitutes, tossing and mumbling in semi-sleep and followed Detective Tyewells into the Detective's Room. One of the Negro detectives was shouting in Spanish at a small Puerto Rican who regarded him blankly. Then he turned and said to no one in particular: "That bastard pretends he can't understand *my Spanish!*" He sounded insulted.

"Look," Tyewells said to me, leaning down. He was a tremendously powerful looking man. "That woman in there got stuff on her. You ever see 'H'?"

"No. Well, you know, in the Academy. In the display case."

"Yeah," Tyewells said, in some effort at patience. "Well, this is not the Academy, and she got the stuff on her, because if she don't, then what we got us here is a bunch of irate citizens. You know?" Tyewells took a deep breath and seemed sorry somehow that I was present.

"Now, look, they teach you how to make a good search? I mean a *good search?*"

Detective Tyewells' eyes sought some sign of recognition, of assurance from my face. I had a vague impression that he was trying to be delicate; he didn't know he sounded patronizing. "If she has the 'H' on her," I said coldly, "you'll be the first to know!"

Tyewells made some kind of sound, a noise halfway between a groan and a laugh, and he tipped his hat as I walked past him and entered the smaller room.

The Irish detective, Quileen, was leaning against the desk, his eyes riveted on the woman.

"She hasn't had a chance to dump it. We didn't leave her out of our sight. Make it good," he said, and left.

The woman was a small, drab-skinned Puerto Rican with long, stringy, dirty black hair. She was smoking a cigarette, and she cupped the ashes into the palm of her hand neatly, then dumped the accumulation to the floor without looking at the grayish snowflakes. I thought for a moment, trying to remember the procedure. You patted a man down for a weapon. They said other policewomen would tell us how to search a female prisoner. But somehow, no one ever had.

"Do you speak English?" I asked.

The woman shrugged, not answering me, but it was apparent that she had understood me. "Okay, I'm Policewoman Uhnak. I have to search you. It would be easy all around if you'd just hand it over now." I waited for a moment, hoping, oh God, how I was hoping, that she would slip a hand inside her dress and hand me a neat little package, and that would be that. The woman regarded me without expression, the way someone with no affinity whatever for cats would regard a Siamese.

"All right, then." I took a deep breath. "Strip."

If the word was a shock to my own mind, it registered only as a command. For the woman, in fantastic response, calmly stood up, slipped out of her shoes and shrank down even smaller than she had seemed. Not looking at me, but not ignoring my eyes, in concentration on her task, she fumbled and pulled at the zipper of her black dress, which was much too long for her. She let the dress fall to the floor, then bent and tossed it on the chair, then unhooked her stockings which were streaked with runs. Then, casually and without any visible emotion, she slipped off her panty girdle and bra. Her underwear was filthy from long use and no washing. She stood there naked and unconcerned in front of me, a slight smile on her mouth; my face must have shown the burning redness I could feel.

I indicated the garments she had strewn about the floor and chair. "Pick them up, one at a time, and shake them over here, over the desk." I didn't want to touch anything from her body. And now, watching her, knowing nothing would fall from her clothing, I knew what Detective Tyewells had meant. I probably had known the minute he had said it, but my mind had rejected the necessity. *A good search.*

The woman was amused by my discomfort, and I gritted my teeth and pushed her away from the desk, then pulled my hand back. It felt diseased and unclean.

"All right," I said, "the game is over. Hand over the 'H.' "

The woman's mouth stretched, showing the four gold front teeth, and then she flung a lank strand of black hair over her thin shoulder and, grinning, twisted her body obscenely. "You want it, cookie," she leered, "you come and get it!"

Shock and anger are closely related: one can be turned into the other and used for the other. She apparently did not realize that my anger was anything deeper than annoyance, or even arrogance. "You put that little package of 'H' on the table, lady, or I will throw you out that window!"

Her smile faded immediately, and she shrugged.

"H'okay, h'okay, police-lady, you don't need to get tough."

And she produced the cylinder from her secret hiding place and put it on the desk.

"Open it," I said.

There were eight little packets of white powder encased

in plastic envelopes on the desk. "Get dressed," I said, turning from her, unable to look at her again.

I felt a steady, grinding nausea, an urge to run from the room. I didn't want to see her sallow, thin face or to share further in the viewing of her body. There was something so dreadful about a woman who would unprotestingly disrobe when told to do so, a woman who had no feelings about revealing gray, dirty underwear to hostile eyes. Who felt no sense of degradation when ordered to do a degrading thing, but who did so without a flicker of emotion, with nothing showing in her eyes, nothing twitching at her lips. And I didn't like the feeling of being in a position to say "strip" or "dress," to have this power over a person, this authority. It was a mutual humiliation, and I felt my part heavily and with disgust. This was a woman totally without hope, and she had revealed herself to me with no feelings about herself, just as though it didn't matter; and so nothing mattered, nothing meant anything to her.

She didn't ask for help with her zipper, and though I knew she was struggling, arms bent at jagged angles, I was unwilling to touch her, to touch any part of her. My hand was still conscious, like a separate living thing, of the one brief contact with her shoulder.

Tyewells was right outside the door, and he entered immediately when I looked out. "Eight packets," I said. He regarded me, looking for something in my face, his own a mask of brown, intelligent amusement. He nodded, then held up his hand to Lieutenant Bouvreau across the room. His index finger and thumb formed a circle.

"We got it. Everyone can relax. The 'H' is here." Then Tyewells nodded to me curtly, but it was a kind of approval. Okay, kid, okay.

The remainder of my tour was relatively quiet. I spent midnights to mornings in my small office listening to my prisoners singing softly to themselves, quarreling across the bars, complaining, sobbing, sleeping fitfully, snoring, coughing, cursing. I was getting the feel of them; the strong physical sense of their misery and hopelessness was rubbing into my skin like a tangible thing, like a warm, sticky, unclean liquid. I could feel the oppressive air of internment, of confined women, grinding into me with a terrible intensity. They were only detained here overnight, these dreadful, wasted women, to face court in the morning and probably a more definite term of imprisonment. They spent just one night here, but I felt like I was serving time in my own special cell. I couldn't stop myself from looking at them, at their faces, at their eyes reflecting years of living and time spent in ways foreign and strange and incomprehensible to me. I tried speaking to them. I let them use me for the small, insignificant favors that were so vital to them, now, in this place. I gave them combs, Kleenex, cigarettes, coffee, candy. In talking to them, I tried to trace some pattern to lives which otherwise seemed governed by an insane and shapeless fate.

Sitting at my desk, drinking the endless cups of tea to keep me awake through the nights, I could feel their scorn, their hatred and contempt and bitterness, not directed at me, but at everyone and everything in their world which had put them in this place where a comb or a clean paper cup was important and meaningful.

These were the things I hadn't known. These were the people I hadn't known. It wasn't like in the movies at all. It was a slow-moving, steady, repetitious monotony. Even the Friday and Saturday nights of activity when the Detective Squad Room was filled with people had a sameness: complainants wailing in anxiety or outrage; suspects glowering, sullen, or protesting, frightened; mothers of sons, asking plaintively, "Where is he? What did you do with him?" and detectives answering, "You should have asked that before, lady. You should have worried about where he was before."

And I knew, now, that the special atmosphere of a police precinct was made up of these things: of an anguish and a despair that hangs in the air as thick as the cigarette smoke and as stained as the coffee containers.

And that all detectives, those in the Harlem precinct and those of my childhood fantasies, all detectives, no matter what their color or size or shape, they all have the same eyes: hard and knowing.

3

*"You will build a hard,
impenetrable wall around yourself"*

I can't understand why any policewoman would want to
be permanently assigned to the office of the Policewomen's
Bureau. About the only advantage is that you work a
steady tour and get more week ends off. Outside of that,
it is nothing more than an office job. Taking phone calls,
typing up reports of interviews with complainants, keeping
work schedules, filing—all the dull, deadly, systematically
bland routines I have always encountered with a sense of
annoyance and resentment bordering on desperation. Yet,
I learned that the women on such permanent assignment
considered themselves a kind of elite little band. But they
could keep it. After my tour of matron duty, I was assigned
to the Bureau for my 8 to 4 tour and kept at a desk. It
was good to be home in time to prepare dinner for Tony,
and for us to be able to go to a movie together, or just
for a walk and to know that our evenings were our own.
That was for a week.

On my 4 P.M. to 12 midnight tour the following week,
I was assigned to work with a partner, May Evans. She
was a woman in her late thirties, with blondish hair and
eyebrows and a thin face. May had a singular look of
competence; it was evident in her manner, her way of
talking brusquely and with some humor and without wast-
ing words. Everything was sharp and clean-cut and without
adjectives.

May led me around Manhattan: a kind of guided tour,
showing me things I hadn't seen before. Not the skating
rink at Rockefeller Center, but the shifting crowd that
watched the diners aimlessly, for the weather was too
warm for ice skaters. She pointed out, quickly, sharply,

surely. "Him, with the brown suit, watch him." And sure enough, the man would move into a group of women, closer, then move out again, seemingly without purpose, and we would come up close behind him and notice those things about him: a certain grayish cast to his lips, a certain vacant look in his eyes which focused on space, a certain lack of expression, a blankness about him as he dreamed his own fantastic dreams of pleasure, triggered by his brushing, casual contact with the clothing or hip or shoulder of some woman tourist.

"Bumper," May said briskly. "That's what we call him —that's what he does. One of the garden variety: he presses against them, and most women just think it's a little crowded and will move away, or maybe not even notice him. Then he gets a little more brazen, maybe causing a woman to turn around and look at him. He'll be staring off, and the woman will think she imagined it or maybe give him a dirty look, or move, and he'll just drift off to another crowd."

"What do we do about it?" I didn't remember any section about "bumpers" in the Penal Code.

May laughed, a short intaking of breath. "Depends. If he is a real desperado, we go after him. Keep him under observation, keep track of his moves—you know, give him enough rope. When we decide we have enough, we can pick him up on 'dis-con' 722-1 or 2, but it's a lousy pinch and it's tough to make it stick. In court, he'll say he was on his lunch hour, which is probably true; that he works across the street—true again; that he was just spending some time in the sunshine."

"So we really haven't got him on anything."

"Well," May said, "if we are very lucky, which we rarely are, we might get some indignant woman, someone he really got fresh with, who is willing to be the complainant. Or, he might take a fancy to one of us—you because you're small, me because I'm ten pounds overweight. We let him come to us, we don't set ourselves up for a creep like this. It's too dirty. Say he thinks I'm nice, likes my broad beam," she patted her hip quickly, "or likes my blue dress—it reminds him of Mother. So he uses me as his target, making contact with me. Taking into consideration his various moves, we bag him. I'm the complainant on action, not just on observation." May sighed. "Of course, he'd probably beat us in court anyway. Then again, we watch a guy, see all his moves, and we just might get him exposing himself, right out here in the open, only really in secret, in the crowd, because who would ever even notice him?"

We made a tour of midtown movies, the big flashy first-runs and the crummy, scratchy ones that were filled with people trying to pass time in their lives, to fill the emptiness with something, hoping for some miracle to be shown them on the large gray screen. But we didn't watch any of the pictures: we watched the people. We sat in the back of the theater and May said, "Him." She spotted them instantly—the "seat-hoppers."

"He made a move when we first came in, did you notice?"

I hadn't, of course.

"Now watch. There he goes. Keep your eye on him—I'll give him about ten minutes."

In less time than that, the black figure moved again. I had noticed a "seat-hopper" of my own, a bulky, lumbering figure who grunted up the aisle, then returned, crackling candy wrappers, to search the rows of seats.

"He's just a hungry one," May said. "I bet fatso won't move again until he runs out of nourishment."

She was right. May explained the "seat-hoppers": "They fit into several categories. Some will sit behind a woman who has an empty seat next to her. Women are notoriously careless about their pocketbooks; at least half the women in a movie will put their coat and pocketbook on an empty seat next to them. They figure it's safe, there's no one near them. They don't think about the guy in the row behind, who just tips the seat, gets the pocketbook, removes the wallet and good-by. Then, of course, there is our friend, the degenerate who hops around the theater making new contacts. The minute he sits down, he stares at the screen and starts operating real slow, just a leg a little closer. You know the type, you're a woman, you've gone to the movies alone."

Yes, and you sit there, feeling strangely uncomfortable, but also slightly guilty. Imagining it, you push your foot against his, just testing; he moves away a tiny bit, and you are satisfied. But still, there is some peculiar feeling, and he persists and you can feel, not exactly feel, but sense the pressure, the warmth, the something wrong. Finally, you are sure—shocked sure—and you either get up indignantly, stamping on his foot as you go, or give him one hard kick, if you have the nerve. Then he takes off wordlessly, and slinks about the movie house for another seat.

I came home from these 4 to 12s exhausted but at the same time exhilarated, telling Tony these things—these things that were there all the time and that I was just now learning to see. It was like focusing on the fascinating culture of ants or bees, being caught up in the minutiae that put everything else out of line.

"See that man?" I would say when we went to a movie to see a picture. "Watch him."

Tony would sink down in his seat. "You know, I can't enjoy a movie any more with you. He's going to the bathroom. Relax and watch the picture."

But he would be caught up in it too, and by the third move, would poke me. "What do you think he is—degenerate or bag opener?"

Improving his vision, through me, Tony would come in furious from his subway ride home. "There was this miserable 'bumper' and this poor dopey kid; she must have been unconscious not to feel him. I wedged myself against him, and when the door opened at 14th Street, I shoved him out. You should have seen him scramble for another door."

On our last 4 to 12, May was at the office before me for the first time.

"You know something," I said, "I've got a feeling we're going to break the ice tonight." Two of the other girls I had graduated with had made their first pinches. I was still waiting, and I had a feeling that tonight would be different. It was.

May didn't look up from the slip of paper, and she spoke with a cigarette dangling from her lips. "We have a special assignment. We have to take some kids to the Foundling Hospital."

I felt a little silly and embarrassed at her complete failure to give any credence to my "feeling"; she had ignored my words and finished her note-taking. A plain-clothesman drove us up to East Harlem. After two weeks away from the neighborhood, the vital, exciting, real, modern, sense-of-going-somewhere atmosphere of mid-Manhattan had almost obliterated the oppression of those dark garbage streets. The driver pulled up alongside a bright red fire chief's car which was parked in front of a fire hydrant. The driver, a gray-haired fireman, nodded solemnly at us, then went on reading his magazine.

The building was a tenement, different from its neighbors only because of the smoky, charred odor and the groups of curious people, dark-eyed, excited and nervous. At every landing in the hallway, groups of tenants were gathered, some looking down the stairwell to the third floor, others craning their necks upward.

"Pin your shield on your jacket," May said, and I noticed hers was already on.

Firemen were talking to people, entering the various flats, checking things off on long sheets attached to clipboards, trying to make themselves understood, following that age-old absurdity that if you talk English loud enough, anyone can understand you.

The odor was thick on the third floor. Mixed with the smell of smoke and wet dirt there was another odor, an alarming odor that was at once familiar and known, yet never encountered before.

There were four doors on the landing, three of them open, filled with people, large-eyed, dark-skinned, small, narrow-boned and talking incessantly in Spanish. May spoke to a fireman who was still wearing his heavy rubber coat and boots, the large cumbersome hat hiding most of his face. I noticed that the people in the doorway seemed to be staring at one corner of the landing, a blackish, dry spot. The tall fireman walked over to me with May, and all I could see of his face was a square jaw and a wide mouth.

"The kids are in there, Apartment 7, with a Mrs. Santiago. Two little ones, the girl is about four months old, the other, the boy, is three years old. The dead ones were four and five years old." He said it flatly, and his face was pointed to that corner; then he walked away.

May looked at me, her face calm and relaxed. "The bodies are gone. Relax. Come on, let's go get the others."

I knew where the burned bodies had lain, and what the peculiar odor was, and I tried to avoid that corner, which drew my eyes like a magnet.

Mrs. Santiago was standing in the doorway with her husband and three little children, and they moved aside with many fluttering, nodding motions, extending their arms into their home for us.

"Sit, please, please take this chair," Mrs. Santiago said, removing a small girl who was leaning against the old straight kitchen chair. "The little ones," she said, her eyes darting toward another room, "they are in there. I dressed them in some warm clothes. I dressed them in my babies' clothes." She said it carefully, her eyes on my face, her head nodding.

"Please, er, lady, please," Mr. Santiago spoke. "I don't speak so good English. Please, lady, what you do with the kids?"

"We are going to take them to the Foundling Hospital. They'll be okay." May's voice sounded harsh against their soft sounds, and she didn't even look at them, but lighted a cigarette, ignoring, or not seeing, Mr. Santiago's effort to dig a match from his pants pocket.

"You like some coffee?" Mrs. Santiago leaped to her stove, which was next to a small sink. This apparently was the kitchen-living room, for there was a sofa and television set against one wall.

May looked up at me. Her face reflected her distaste: she wouldn't touch anything in this room. She shook her head and began making entries in her memo book.

"No, thank you, Mrs. Santiago, I don't drink coffee."

One of the small boys, with tremendous eyes and a runny nose, was regarding me over the top of the table. I smiled at him, and he retreated to his mother's skirt, peeking shyly out at me.

"We have to wait for the sergeant; he'll be back in a minute," May said to me, ignoring the people whose home we were in.

It seemed hours before we heard a commotion in the hallway. The firemen were clearing out the last of their equipment, and we heard a shrill voice scream hysterically. May motioned to me to stay where I was, and she went into the hallway. I watched her talking to the sergeant and to a tiny woman with wild hair and a bright red-purple dress. I could feel the hair on my arms tingle and a chill go down my spine. May put her hands on the woman's shoulders and held her against the wall, and the woman twisted violently from side to side, her voice piercing like razors rubbed on glass. Then she seemed to slide down, as though her legs were rubber, but May pulled her up again, and the woman stopped screaming and was gesticulating and talking in a combination of Spanish and English. When I turned and surprised Mrs. Santiago, who was watching me, she smiled, but it was a heavy, weighted smile, an automatic smile. She turned in what seemed desperation to a little girl about seven years old.

"Carmen," she said, "give the lady some pretzels."

The child silently offered me a tall stick of pretzel from a plastic water tumbler, and I thanked her and took a dry, sticking bite.

May came back, ignoring the Santiagos, and sat down at the table. "The son of a bitch," she said. "The crummy little son of a bitch."

"Was that the . . . the mother?"

May looked up at me, her mouth tight and narrow. "Yeah, I guess you could call her that. You know what that was all about? Well, listen, kiddo, and learn something. That bitch out there was out all night, making her living. She left those kids alone, and they found some matches and set themselves on fire. Two of her kids are dead, and do you know what's bugging her? Hold onto your hat. The ones who are dead, well, she was getting Welfare checks for them. The others, the ones in there, well, her 'husbands' are responsible for making regular payments. She got a court order, but of course they don't come through. The fathers of the two dead ones are in Puerto Rico," she slurred the last words, her sarcasm heavy and mean, "so Welfare paid for them. And do you know what that slob out there wanted the sergeant to do? Guess, go ahead, guess."

I couldn't imagine, but May didn't wait for me to try; she spoke so matter-of-factly, assuming that I would have guessed it anyway.

"That's right. She wanted the sergeant to put in the report that it was the other two who got killed, who burned to death, so that Welfare would go on with the payments. 'What's gonna hoppen to *me?*' That's what she said. 'What's gonna hoppen to *me?*' "

Even the smallest child in the room, though not comprehending her words, was frightened by her face, which was contorted and furious. She turned abruptly to Mrs. Santiago. "All right, get the two of them ready. We're going to take them now."

Mrs. Santiago bobbed up and down, with a kind of bowing motion, and rushed into the other room. She came back carrying a small pink bundle and holding the hand of a little boy with long black hair falling in ragged bangs over his eyes. His eyes were black and wide but tearless, and he walked with her soundlessly.

"Raymond," she said softly. "This is Raymond." And she stood, hesitantly, not sure where she was to entrust the child. "And the little one, she sleeps, is Conchita."

I put my hand out and Raymond came to me, but May stood up. "You take the infant. Come on, sonny." The little boy went immediately to May and put his hand out. She arranged her pocketbook and scraps of paper; then, without looking at him, she reached her hand behind her, and the little boy trailed along.

"Listen, you people," May said, turning at the doorway, her face hard, her voice ugly and cruel. "This is what happens when you go out all night and leave these kids alone. You hear?"

Mr. Santiago's slender body was rigid and his dark eyes blazed with some strong feeling. He swallowed hard, but his voice was soft and broken.

"The fireman, he came and said this to us. We never do such a thing." His voice had taken on a different quality: not exactly of defiance, but more like pride. "My wife, no work. She stay home with the kids." And then, seeing May's unmoving face, his voice wavered. "My wife," he said, turning to the small woman at his side, "she saved these two. She went into the fire and she took these . . . these two out!"

May regarded him blankly, with no indication of having heard his words or seen his face. "Yeah," she said, walking into the hallway, not turning back, *"you* never do such a thing. *Not you!"*

Mr. Santiago's slender body trembled, his mouth tightened. I held the baby in my arms and started toward the door.

"These little ones," Mrs. Santiago said, "I dressed them in *my babies' clothes*. They can keep them. You don't have to bring them back." It was no small sacrifice.

The plea was etched into her small face: We are not like that one out there. I am a mother, not she. Her face was soft and sorrowful, the eyes pained and sensitive.

"Yes, Mrs. Santiago. Thank you." I waited a moment, then the words tumbled out. "You . . . you are a good woman. I mean that."

They said nothing, and perhaps I had offended them, giving them *my* blessing and *my* judgment, but I didn't know what else to say.

We passed the mother of the dead children in the hallway, and May said a few brisk words in Spanish to her. But the woman didn't answer or look at the child as he walked past her, sucking his thumb, or at the sleeping baby in my arms.

In the car, May stood the boy up by the window and he gazed silently out at the street.

"These people," May said. "Boy, these goddamn people, they should have stayed where the hell they came from."

I put my finger to my lips, nodded toward the boy.

"Him?" she said. "No speaka English." And she stared past the boy's head, not touching the child with any part of her.

The little boy said something in Spanish, in a high-pitched, babyish voice. May shook her head and answered him briefly.

"I didn't know you spoke Spanish."

"Hunter College special," she said, and this surprised me because none of the rough edges had been honed, none of the finish was there. "He wants to go to the bathroom —he'd better wait."

The child began rocking back and forth from one foot to the other, humming to himself.

I looked at the infant in my arms. Her skin was a delicate beige, her nose tiny and her small lips, pursed in sleep, moved in and out in a sucking motion. "She's a lovely baby," I said, but May didn't seem to hear.

At the Foundling Hospital, a sister led us into the Administration Office. There was a hushed, calm quality in the building. It was a separate world unto itself: safe, apart. The huge headdress of the nuns seemed to frighten Raymond, and he leaned heavily against May's legs as she sat on the chair. She pushed the boy's shoulder and he stood upright, jiggling. The Mother Superior took down all the details without comment, then spoke into an intercom on her desk and another nun appeared, dressed in a crisp white habit.

The boy was staring at the huge crucifix over the Mother Superior's head, sucking on his thumb in loud gasps. The Mother Superior said, "This is Raymond. Raymond, say good-by to the nice ladies and go with Sister Margaret Mary. She will give you a nice supper." Her voice was flat and even.

The boy stiffened as the nun approached, and he looked around the room, his eyes wide and shimmering.

"Come," the sister said softly. "We will give you some nice scrambled eggs, Raymond. Do you like scrambled eggs?" Raymond began chewing on his thumb. The sister smiled. "Don't eat the thumb, child. I'll give you some food."

"He doesn't understand English," I said, still holding the sleeping infant.

The Mother Superior nodded. "We have sisters here who speak Spanish. He will be fine."

"He has to go to the bathroom," I said.

The Mother Superior smiled, tapping a pencil on her desk. "It is routine, Policewoman Uhnak. Bathroom, hands and faces washed, light supper and sleep. He will be fine."

Raymond, tears sliding down his cheeks but soundless, took hold of the sister's long flowing garb, and she reached for the baby. I stood up, looking at the tiny, unguarded face. "She's asleep, sister. She's been asleep the whole time." And still I held the child and the sister patiently waited.

May stood up suddenly and pulled the infant from my arms and thrust her at the nun. The jolting transfer startled the infant and there was a sharp intake of breath and then an indignant cry from the small bundle. "Come on, Uhnak, she isn't yours and we don't have all night!"

I could have killed her then, at that moment. In this quiet, peaceful place, founded on and filled with unquestioning devotion, I felt a greater urge toward physical violence than I knew I possessed, and I didn't answer her or even hear the Mother Superior bidding us good-by.

When we got back in the car, the driver glanced over his shoulder at me in the rear seat. "Plenty room up front."

I shook my head and he shrugged and started the car. May was talking to him. They were deciding where to go: Chinatown for chop suey or to an Italian joint. They decided on the Italian joint. I sat at the table with them, listening to them go over the menu, evaluating one dish against another, selecting a nice red wine, looking at their watches to judge how long we had. The driver excused himself to make a ring, and May pushed the menu at me, but I shoved it hard back at her. Our eyes were riveted on one another.

May took a deep breath and put the menu down and put her palm flat on it. "All right," she said, her voice low and irritated. "It was a stinker. The whole night, the whole thing, the whole bit." And then tightly, through clenched teeth, accusingly, "I was there, too, remember?"

"Were you?"

For the first time, some trace of emotion came to her voice, some signs of life. "Oh, yes, Dorothy. I was there, too. Every minute of it and every step of the way. But there was one big difference. You see, I've learned a trick. Be my guest, benefit from my vast and superior experience. A very simple trick. Just this—you never look at their eyes. You never look at their faces." She looked down at her hands, straightened the fingers out, then looked back at me. "You see, in that way, they can't haunt you. You can't remember what they look like, and so you forget them. Just like that!" She snapped her fingers almost in my face. "Voices are very easy to forget, and words—they don't mean a goddamn thing. Don't look at their eyes and you're home safe. Now, are you going to order something or are you going to sit there and watch us make pigs of ourselves?"

I ordered ravioli and ate a little of it and drank two glasses of the wine and got very dizzy, and May typed up our report at the office before we went home.

Tony was half asleep when I got home, and I talked him awake, trying to tell him about it—how it was. He listened quietly, understanding my need to put it into words, to try and get it all out, to purge myself of it.

"I have to look in their eyes," I said. "Isn't it stupid—I can't help it. I have to carry it all around with me."

He said all the comforting words that had no meaning, that didn't penetrate. There was just the sound of his voice, concerned, weary, trying. It wasn't much, but it was enough. It was all there was.

The next night, I was off duty and we went to some friends' house for a social evening. Our host, an enthusiastic, energetic long-time friend, introduced us to another couple we hadn't met before.

"And I'd better warn you," he said, smiling, "Dotty is a real honest-to-God policewoman—carries a gun and everything!"

The girl hunched forward, brightly eager for some new experience, to hear some exciting inside stories.

The man, a carefully groomed, well-made collegiate type in his thirties, grinned knowingly. His name was Marty and he said, arching his eyebrows: "Listen, I know about cops. I know all about you cops!"

Tony passed a wordless message to me—of sympathy, complete and whole.

"Do you really?" I said coldly. "Marty, you don't know anything."

And I proceeded to be a very poor guest: a silent, uncommunicative guest, much to my host's dismay, for I had apparently been heralded as a good storyteller.

But I told them nothing.

4

"I shall serve the law; I shall serve the people"

In my first few months as a police officer, I had been almost totally removed from the main functions of the police: prevention of crime, detection and apprehension of criminals. I had seen apprehended persons once they were in detention, but I had not taken an active part in what I considered the *real* job of the police. So I was filled not only with anticipation but with a good deal of apprehension when I was assigned to work with a detective in the Bronx.

Bill Bayreuth was a tall, lanky, monosyllabic man with a face as creased and reddened as old leather. He looked like a cowboy and carried himself with a slouching long step as though his feet resented the pavements and he were searching for flat space. He was the kind of man who didn't speak unless he had something to say, and since he had nothing to say, he was for the most part silent. When we met the group of high school girls outside the main entrance of the all-girls school in the Bronx, he told me, partly in abrupt gestures and partly in quick grunts, where he would be, what our signals were, and what our procedure was to be.

I stood with the group of five girls, a part of them. When I had been a high school girl, we had worn moccasins and white bobby socks, a little lipstick and a fresh, clean look: we had looked young. These girls were all sixteen years old, all remarkably similar in their dress, hair style, make-up and their long disheveled bangs painstakingly arranged to touch the corners of their pale-shadowed eyelids which were heavy with eyeliner. Their lips were blanked out with pale lipstick, and they all looked wan and tubercular. Dressed smartly, their feet easy in medium-height pumps, their manner belied the outward sophistication. Their faces were animated and they spoke in bursts of giggles, dangerously close to hysteria. Hearing their voices, their gasps of breath and words, I felt somehow very old, though there were not that many years between us. I had never realized sixteen was so young, and I wondered if I had sounded like that, if I had been given to shrill and unexpected bursts of senseless, irrational gasps of laughter followed immediately by serious, almost solemn composure.

"Policewoman Uhnak, do you think he'll show up today?"

They all became silent, mouths opening, eyes focusing on my face intently.

"Well, I think we'll just wait and see." I was sure I sounded just like one of their teachers, so old and wise and calm and patient. "But remember, please, don't any of you do anything. My partner and I will take care of it." That sounded fine: nothing to worry about.

They all nodded, seeming to gain reassurance from my attitude toward the situation. The girls all had that sharp sense of here and now—a keen awareness of the moment, a feeling of excitement and at the same time dread. I shared this feeling but knew it must be concealed from them, because their control would reflect my own. They were leaning on me fully, without question. Strangely enough, this gave me a certain confidence.

"My mother was a wreck this morning," announced one girl, blowing a strand of black hair from her mouth. "Why, she didn't want me to come to school today, but I told her *I had to.*"

The others nodded, and it seemed that all the mothers had had the same idea. We had sat with the mothers and some of the fathers the night before, in the home of one of the parents, a doctor. They had all described, with strong emotions, the molestations their daughters had suffered at the hands of the man we were awaiting. They had all been quite verbal and vehement, and some of the fathers, comfortably seated in back of a coffee table laden with expensive pastry, had threatened to take matters into their own hands. Wives had reached beautifully manicured hands to the abundant, thick masculine shoulders and admonished restraint. Bill had explained that their daughters would be under police protection; that they would all be asked to come to court, after we apprehended the man, to press complaints, and that in all likelihood the culprit would plead guilty; they had nothing whatever to worry about. The parents had agreed to have the girls meet us at school, had agreed to follow through with complaints. And yet, each mother, this morning, had tried to keep her own daughter at home.

Looking at these girls, I could guess what their arguments had been: "But mother, I don't want to be the only one left out!"

One of the girls, a short, slightly plump dumpling with dark horn-rimmed glasses, stiffened suddenly and held her head very still. Her voice was low and a perfect imitation of a television actress noticing her next door neighbor using the wrong detergent. "He's coming! I just saw his car turn the corner."

The girl with the black hair pushed her bangs from her forehead and peeked out. "I can't stand it!" she said flatly.

"Now look, girls, that's what we're here for. My partner has spotted him, too. Now please, let's just relax."

There was a tightening sensation in my throat, as though that long tube inside my neck was shrinking. Bill, across the street, leaning languidly against a street lamp, had his face in his newspaper. I wasn't sure that he had seen my signal.

My own annoyance at the sudden fidgeting and dramatics of the teenagers, who were living their own excitement at top pitch, held the flash of panic deep inside me and gave me something to concentrate on—something to distract me from my own tenseness.

In a few moments, the man came along the street toward us. I had memorized the descriptions the girls had given and had formed my own mental image of him, and I was certain I would be able to pick him out of a crowd. He would be seedy and sly, and the degeneracy of his acts would affect his whole physical appearance. He would walk with a certain slouch, a certain sidling, lurching, unwholesome step. It would be all about him, covering him like an unmistakable cloak. His actual appearance was a valuable lesson. He was, as they had told us, a redheaded man. He was not, as they had told us, or as I had imagined, some stereotyped caricature monster. He was just a slightly built, youngish redhead, of medium height, with glasses. He was neatly dressed in a gray jacket and gray trousers. He could come to your door each morning with milk or bread, or sell you watches behind a counter or drive your bus or be your cousin's husband. His appearance came as a shock. He was living proof of what they had tried to teach the recruits at the Academy: John Doe is an ordinary looking man capable of murder, arson, theft, sodomy or any of the other crimes specified in the Penal Code.

"Are any of you going to the dance Saturday night?" They all stared at me as though I had gone mad. "I have a dream of a date, a boy named Tony. Did I tell you about Tony?"

The short blonde made some kind of moaning noise, and I spoke directly to her, holding onto her with my voice, warning her. "He is the sweetest boy I've ever known, sort of blondish, and that's funny because I always thought I liked dark men better."

"I used to go with a blond boy," said the girl with the long bangs. She nodded her head and spoke quickly, her voice high-pitched. I was grateful to her, and she continued speaking. "I forget his name though, I just can't remember." She broke off with a giggle.

I kept talking, holding us all together, fully aware of their feelings, fully sharing them.

The redheaded man was leaning against the fence, about fifteen feet away from us.

"Oh, God," said the blonde, her eyes wild. "I can't stand it!"

"Tony isn't very tall, but he has blue eyes and high cheek bones and one of those soft, deep voices and . . ."

The blonde moaned again. "He's suspicious," she said

in a loud whisper. "We always move away when he comes. He knows something's funny, he knows."

"Keep still. You just stand there and keep quiet and don't move."

One of the girls standing next to me jabbed me with her elbow and I almost dropped the armload of schoolbooks. "He's doing it," she said, "he's exposing himself."

Before I could say anything, the girls all turned and looked at him, and then at me, and they began making the laughing-crying sounds, and my voice was firmer and more certain than I was. "Turn around and look at me and keep talking." They reacted, grateful for a command, and I brushed my hand over my hair and did not look past their faces, for the man was directly in my line of vision. "My partner is walking across the street. No, turn and look at me, face me, you dope, or he'll run. You just stand here and don't do a thing." I saw Bill's approach, saw him spin the man toward him, holding his arm. "Okay, kids, that's it. I just want you to come over with me now and identify him to his face."

I held the blonde's arm, and the others trailed along reluctantly. Bill had the redhead up against the fence and was leaning against him slightly. His clothes had been zipped and the girls, one by one, glanced at him quickly, murmured "Yes," then moved away.

"We're going to book him at the precinct for indecent exposure now, and I'll call you all tonight and let you know when you and your mothers are to come to court. All right?" They all nodded at me and, relieved and anxious to get away, they moved off in a group. Silent at first, they finally burst into hysterical chattering, turning to watch us over their shoulders as they hurried on, eager to spread the excitement to other classmates across the street.

My hand shook as I lit a cigarette and went up to the prisoner. His face was without expression, and his eyes blinked steadily behind the dirty, finger-smudged, rimless glasses. He had a small, round nose and ruddy cheeks; the skin around his eyes and mouth was a network of delicate wrinkles, the kind of skin a midget has, smooth yet crumpled at the same time. His hands hung limply at his sides, and he seemed neither nervous nor arrogant nor upset. He seemed to be in a kind of trance, to have removed himself from the situation, with his eyes focused on another time or place. Bill was questioning him, and he was answering in monosyllables, flatly, just audibly.

"This young lady is a police officer. Did you know that when you exposed yourself to her and the other girls?"

The man blinked a few more times, rhythmically. "No. I didn't expose myself."

"We're arresting you for indecent exposure," I said, not too sure if I should say anything at all.

"No," he said, without emotion.

"You've been hanging around this school a lot, haven't you?"

He regarded Bill blankly. "No."

"You've been saying some pretty bad things to those girls, haven't you? And doing some pretty nasty things to them?"

He was facing Bill, but seemed to be studying something beyond him. "No," he said, without protest. It was just a meaningless word in his mouth.

"Well, they say you have. They say you've been grabbing them and feeling them, and doing all kinds of things to them."

The man was silent for a moment and then, "My brother's a cop," he said, the way a child would say it, with pride.

Bill stiffened for a moment, stopped by this announcement. His eyes screwed up, and he spoke with the cigarette sticking to his lips. "Yeah? Where's he work?"

The man looked surprised. "In New York City."

"Yeah, sure. In New York City. What precinct."

"My brother's a cop," the man said, insistently.

"Great," Bill said. "Now you just show me your identification, and we're going to take a ride to the police station."

"Will we see my brother? He's a cop."

At the precinct, we wrote up the arrest cards. Our

prisoner's name was Phillip Rettick; he was thirty-one years old, unmarried, a clerk, living with his mother.

And, he said, his brother was a cop.

Bill spoke to the lieutenant at the desk. "I don't care if his uncle is the mayor," said Lieutenant Schwartz, "the bum gets locked up." And then he lowered his voice. "Particularly with all those complainants. One of those kids' father is a lawyer, and he was raising hell on the phone yesterday."

The redhead was a cooperative, orderly prisoner, speaking only when asked something, shaking his head when asked about the charges against him, looking puzzled and lost. When we were getting into the patrol wagon which was to take us to police headquarters for photos, then on to court, he stopped, looked at his watch.

"I'll be late," he said.

"For what?"

"For work. Gotta be there by four o'clock."

"Yeah, sure," said Bill, pushing him along into the wagon.

At Felony Court, Rettick was arraigned, and Bill spoke to the assistant district attorney, a short, sandy-haired man with tan-rimmed glasses resting on the bridge of his nose.

"We've got five other complainants. Teen-age girls. I want to rearrest him tomorrow: indecent exposure, simple assault. This bum's been hanging around the school for weeks. The kids finally got around to telling their parents about it."

"Okay," the D.A. said, his head lowered into his chest as he studied papers for the next arraignment. "Sure, we'll ask for an adjournment until tomorrow. You have those girls here."

Bail was set at $1,000, and Rettick, looking vacantly around, said nothing. He walked where Bill led him, and then went with the court attendant, who led him out of sight to the detention cells. Bill brought the commitment papers back, and the judge signed them. Bill signaled for me to meet him in the back of the court, then disappeared into the detention room again.

I sat on the last bench in the courtroom, looking at the

high ceiling and dark paneling of the walls. It was like a huge, hollow cavern, and it wasn't difficult to understand the worried faces of the friends and relatives awaiting the appearance of various prisoners. There was a cold anonymity to the official readings of the offenses being charged. Only the name had any meaning, and then only to those directly involved. The clerk's voice was muffled and unclear, and the words didn't carry beyond the first row or two. The prisoner would stand before the judge. His relative would be straining to make some sense out of the words being read or pulling on the prisoner's arm, or glaring at him, or whispering to him, or weeping quietly, or sobbing noisily—it was all the same—and the reading would go on in the steady sing-song voice that had called out every possible horror in the same even tone. The district attorney would look up from his papers, say something. Words would be exchanged between the bench and the stenographer. An attorney would speak or Legal Aid would be assigned. The relative, usually a wife, would stand, staring, searching for a face to turn to, and her attorney would take her arm or the court attendant would tell her to step back. Her whole world at this instant would be this big, endless grotto of a room, filled with strangers holding their own troubles against their bodies with their arms, avoiding the eyes of anyone else, not willing to share other tragedies or bewilderments or fears. I dropped my eyes as an elderly woman, some mother, wearing a dirty, too-large blue coat and a thick bright kerchief, walked uncertainly down the wide aisle, looking from face to face, searching for direction.

When Bill finally emerged from the wire mesh cage leading to the detention quarters, his face was creased and his lips were taut. "Come on outside, we'll talk there."

We walked to the wide marble chamber of a hallway, where conferences were being held in small, worried groups. Lawyers were insistently instructing destroyed looking relatives, who were hanging hopefully on every word and gesture.

"Jesus," Bill said, "now he tells me his brother is a police captain."

"Is he?"

"Who knows? The guy's a real nut. He acts like he's not with it; you have to watch out for that type. He can snap at any minute. I've had a few like that; I'm glad he's off our hands."

We returned to the precinct to give the desk officer the details of the arraignment, and I dialed the first number on my list of the girls' names. It was the home of the doctor's daughter, since that was where the parents had gathered the previous night.

Mrs. Small's voice was smooth and well-modulated, with a certain warmth and charm that carefully spelled out her position as the wife of a doctor. I remembered her from the night before: she was sharp-featured, a birdlike woman, small-boned with clean dark hair swept back from her narrow face into a sleek, intricately twisted bun, and bright eyes and clear skin.

"Yes, Mrs. Uhnak, Joanne told us about it, and I can't tell you how completely relieved we are. You people certainly did a marvelous job, and I can't tell you how much we appreciate the way you handled it. Protecting our girls, I mean."

"Well, that's our job. Now, I'd like Joanne and the other girls, and you mothers, to meet us in the Complaint Room tomorrow morning at nine-thirty. That's at 100 Centre Street, the Criminal Courts Building, on the second floor and . . ."

The careful voice interrupted. "Of course, our main concern in all of this, quite naturally, is the protection of our girls. It is such a relief to know that this man is behind bars. You realize, of course, my dear, that the girls are at such an impressionable age."

"Yes, of course. Now, we'll be in the Complaint Room before nine-thirty waiting for you, and the procedure is very simple. We'll . . ."

"They are our main concern," the voice reiterated in my ear, "and that is why we're so very grateful and I know that you will understand."

There was a momentary silence. "Understand what, Mrs. Small?" I asked softly, not wanting to admit that I knew, had known from the moment her voice sounded elegantly in my ear.

"Well, of course, we don't want to subject the girls to anything that may harm them, you see. We feel, the other parents and Dr. Small and myself, that the girls have been exposed to enough sordidness. We really feel that to subject them to a courtroom procedure now . . ."

The lightly positive flow of her words weighed me down with a weariness. I hadn't realized how drained and tired I was, not just physically but emotionally, too. It was in an attempt to stimulate myself, to awaken myself, that I tried to fight her. "What do you mean, Mrs. Small? I don't understand."

My voice was louder, cold. Bill stopped writing in his memo book and squinted through the smoke of his cigarette, following my part of the conversation, reading the rest from my face and tapping fingers.

The voice at the other end became a little sharper, edged with some vague hint, some warning. "I am sure you can understand that we will not allow the girls to appear in court as complainants. We feel quite satisfied now that this man has been apprehended and you police officers have taken him into custody. As far as we are concerned, we are very pleased with the results. In fact, Dr. Small is going to write a letter to the police commissioner," she said brightly, "and all the other parents are going to sign it, commending you and your partner for your splendid cooperation and quick action. I'm sure that will be of help to you."

"Mrs. Small, this matter isn't ended yet." Bill was rubbing his long hand over his face, messing up his eyebrows. "We arrested this man for indecent exposure today, but without the other complaints, it might not stand up."

Mrs. Small was very firm now. "Yes, I understand that. But he exposed himself to *you.* None of the children saw it today."

"They were standing with me, of course they saw it. They all saw it."

And now Mrs. Small's voice was final, not open to argument. "No, my dear, they did not. We feel, all the parents feel—and I should tell you that three of the other mothers are right here with me"—she paused momentarily, and I could see the three other mothers nodding their heads up and down righteously—"that this is quite an adequate action. We are satisfied with this man's arrest on your charges."

"Mrs. Small . . ."

"As I said, we do not want this to have too much of an effect on our young daughters. We feel that pursuing this any further will be detrimental to their psychological well-being, because they are so impressionable."

"Don't you think it might make a very strong and very good impression on them to come into court and see for themselves that a man who has been molesting them and exposing himself to them for weeks was arrested the first time they reported it to the police, and that they have police officers to turn to when something like this happens?" I ignored Bill's wordless message, his look of resignation and disgust. "Don't you think they are old enough to be reassured that we have police and courts of law for their protection?"

The voice was crisp and brittle now. "I have no intention of arguing with you, Mrs. Uhnak."

"Mrs. Small, last night, when Detective Bayreuth and I spoke with you parents . . ."

"After you and Detective Bayreuth left, we discussed it further. Dr. Small" (she intoned the holy name with the pride of the wife of an expert before an audience of the wives of lesser men) "pointed out the possible harm it might cause the girls to be involved in a courtroom case, and we all decided to let the police handle the matter. After all," the sharp little voice told me, *"it is your job!"*

"Yes. It is our job."

"Well," the voice, triumphant, flashed cheerfully again, "we want to thank you again. Believe me, someday when you're a parent yourself, my dear, you'll understand our feelings."

"Yes," I said, not responding to the wise words which preceded the gentle, final click in my ear.

"Damn it. Damn it. 'Dr. Small says, and Dr. Small thinks.' " I imitated the cool, superior voice.

"And I think I knew it all the time, and we should have hustled those kids right over to the precinct with us." Bill stamped out his juicy cigarette and immediately lit another one. His face was impassive, and he observed my anger without comment.

Bill Bayreuth telephoned me at home after ten that night, and I was surprised to hear his voice. "Listen, Dot, Rettick does have a brother who's a cop."

"So?"

Bill's voice was tight and hard. "So, he's a captain. Captain Rettick, assigned to the commissioner's confidential squad."

I closed my eyes, seeing the nondescript, blank-faced redhead intoning childishly: "My brother's a cop. My brother's a cop."

"And we're going to see Captain Rettick. Tomorrow. We're going to meet him in the luncheonette, you know that greasy-spoon around the corner from the Court? At nine o'clock. Sergeant Gerrity called me just ten minutes ago. I'm going to take some milk for my ulcer now. See you in the morning."

Bayreuth was on his second cup of coffee when I arrived, and the waitress brought the tea I ordered in a thick, scarred, once white cup. The tea bag dangled limply against the side of the cup; I poured in a teaspoon of watery milk and sipped the tepid drink. As I put the cup onto the heavy, cracked saucer, a tall, redheaded man approached the booth. He smiled broadly, and Bill started to rise.

"Bayreuth?" he asked, then held up his hand to tell Bill to remain seated. "And Policewoman Uhnak?"

He slid into the seat next to Bill. He was a tall man with flushed skin, clear green eyes and a slight nervous twitching in the corner of his mouth. Only his red hair related him to his brother. He was well built, with an intelligent, animated face, and was carefully tailored in a dark brown suit, gleaming white shirt and expensive dark tie. There was a small, neat gold tie pin with a replica of his captain's shield midway down the tie. His hands were long and white and narrow, and the blue veins showed through the golden red hairs as he accepted a cigarette that Bill offered him.

"Thank you. Oh, miss, may I have some coffee, please. Black, thank you." He looked around the luncheonette as though he had never seen a luncheonette before, studied the wallpaper, the lighting fixtures, the table top. His beautiful eyes, shaded by long, thick red lashes, darted around with interest. It seemed that he had forgotten why he had come here, or that he had decided not to speak of it after all. And then he turned his eyes on me.

"Well, officer, I think my preliminary remarks should be that I am about as shocked and stunned as a man can be." He shook his head slightly, looking now at his fingers rolling the cigarette around. "I'm sure you can realize my feelings about all this. My brother, I mean."

He raised his arched, fine eyebrows, and I could see remnants of freckles on his forehead. Bayreuth said nothing, studying a shimmering little puddle of coffee about two inches from his cuff.

"Would you mind telling me what happened yesterday? I'd like to know from the moment you arrived at the school."

I told him the circumstances of his brother's arrest, and the captain interrupted several times, crisply and professionally asking the policeman's details. And then there was a silence as the captain seemed to be weighing what he had heard.

"And there was an important detail I haven't covered, Captain."

There was a pressure on my foot and Bayreuth's eyes flashed, but the captain picked it up immediately, not really seeing Bayreuth's face but sensing his signal. He turned to face Bill, and there was light glinting on the tiny golden red hairs along the captain's cheek.

"You tell me, Bayreuth. I must know all the details, you can appreciate that. You see, the major concern in all this, for me, is my brother. To help him, I must know the whole thing."

Bill studied the glistening drop of coffee as though it were something alive waiting to pounce on his sleeve. He mumbled, quickly, that the five girls had been molested and annoyed by the captain's brother for several weeks.

Captain Rettick pressed the cigarette out against the side of his cup and regarded what he had done with distaste, as though he had committed some indiscretion. He sucked his lip thoughtfully, then thrust out his chin. "My God, I had no idea the kid was so bad. You see, I've known for some time that there was something wrong—since he came back from the service. He was in Korea. My kid brother was never what you'd call, well, bright, but he was a good kid. He didn't give you any trouble, did he?"

"No," Bill answered quickly, "no, sir, he was fine."

"I didn't think he had; he's a gentle boy, very timid. He'd never hurt anyone. This business with the girls—are they going to appear against him?"

"No, their mothers won't let them."

The captain let out a long, low whistle of relief at my words. "Thank God for that, anyway. Then it really isn't so bad, is it?" The captain smiled broadly, and his teeth were even and white. "Then it can be fixed up."

The captain was again smiling—a blinding smile, a certain, sure smile that lit up his handsome, boyishly smooth face. "Mrs. Uhnak, I'm sure you can understand my concern for my brother. Believe me, if I had known that he was this sick, I'd have gotten him into the V.A. hospital. That's what I intend to do now. He lives with my mother; God help her, she's seventy years old. I have to protect her from this. I'll tell her it's his stomach; he's had trouble with his stomach in the past. Believe me, he will be taken care of; there will be no possibility of this happening again."

The captain spoke with the easy assurance of one used to taking over, to commanding. He seemed to relax, now that the problem before him had been reduced to a simple statement of solution.

"Captain, just what is it you want us to do?"

He regarded me for a moment, then asked Bill, "You didn't see him expose himself, did you, Bayreuth."

It wasn't a question, it was a flat statement, and Bill affirmed it.

"Good." Now he turned to me. "Mrs. Uhnak, I understand that this is your first arrest."

The knowledge that he had checked up on me, had run me down, was unnerving. "Yes, it is."

"Well, it will be relatively simple, believe me. I intend to protect you fully. There won't be any record in your personnel file of a dismissal, and you'll get full credit for an arrest, so don't worry about that." The captain had a certain charm, a way of using his long golden hands and narrowing his green eyes and lowering his voice to put things in their proper perspective. There was no great problem here: everything was under control. It was a studied, practiced performance. "We'll ask for a hearing, just before lunch break, when there is no one else in court. You see, we'll make it as easy as possible."

I waited, watching him, not saying a word, and he nodded, accepting my silence for compliance.

"We'll get it thrown out, on a reasonable doubt. You'll testify to your affidavit; I wouldn't ask you to change your sworn statement, of course."

My voice was out of rhythm with his, and there was a slight tremor in it. "No prima-facie case? It'll be thrown out?"

The captain threw back his head and laughed out loud for the first time. It was a rich, warm, flowing, young sound and it stopped as unexpectedly as it had begun, but his eyes were still crinkled in humor. "Well, I'm glad to see that some of the instruction at the Police Academy rubbed off on someone. Don't worry about it being thrown out before a prima facie is established. You see, we have made certain, well . . ." He spread his hands on the table. "The district attorney understands the circumstances and the magistrate is an . . . old friend, you might say. The

D.A. will have you testify to your affidavit and that'll be it. Our attorney will lead you into an opening just slight enough to justify, for the record, the reasonable-doubt finding. All legal, simple; you just follow the lead set for you."

He leaned back, so sure, so confident and satisfied and convinced, that the words, unguarded, slipped out. "Do I have a choice?"

His lips twitched; he clenched his hands, flexing the fingers. He saw my face now, *my face,* not a reflection of his own image mirrored on an agreeable image, but his voice was still pleasant. "Wouldn't you expect the same treatment for your own brother, Mrs. Uhnak?"

"I don't have a brother."

"Well, I do."

I ignored the pressure on my foot. Bill was grinding his big shoe on me, but I was fascinated by the change in the color of Rettick's eyes; the green actually faded, paled to a transparent glaze. His cheeks were drawn in, his mouth locked tight and his hands, drawn into tight fists on the table, tapped lightly, just once, indicating that the fact was stated and the matter was closed to further discussion.

And then he relaxed again, the color flowing back into his eyes, and he thrust his hand across the table to me, squeezed my hand hard and shook hands with Bill.

"Mrs. Uhnak, you won't be sorry for this, I promise you. Just testify the way the D.A. and our attorney lead you; it will be very quick and easy. And then, just forget it. But I will remember, believe me. I have an infallible memory." The words sounded threatening, but the tone was pleasant. "You will always have a good friend, and that may come in handy someday."

The good friend smiled warmly, squeezed Bayreuth's shoulder and left.

We sat wordless for a moment. Bill played with a spoonful of cold, tan coffee, letting it trickle into his cup.

"So?"

He looked up at me. "So you do like the man says. Period. The end."

The questioning by the district attorney was brief. He

asked for the facts of the arrest, carefully avoided any mention of the teen-age girls who were present, asked a few questions about distance. Where was he? Where was I? Then he asked me, carefully, if I was positive, absolutely positive, of what I had seen. I found myself hesitating for a split second, heard my voice quaver uncertainly before I answered, "Yes." Did anyone else see this—just answer yes or no. There were "other people" present; I could not say, positively, what they had seen. Did the defendant come along quietly? Yes, he did.

The defense attorney was an amiable man, short with a bald head and bushy eyebrows and a thick mustache. He could afford to be polite to me, and his voice was cordial. Did the defendant deny that he had exposed himself? Yes, he did. Had he come along quietly, cooperatively? Yes, he had. Had he said anything to me or done anything prior to his arrest to gain my atttention? Had he called out, whistled, beckoned? No, he hadn't.

Was I positive, absolutely positive, without the *possibility of some slight, perfectly human mistake,* that I had actually seen him expose himself? I sat there, unable to believe I was hesitating, waiting, and then, softly, in an unknown voice, I said, No I didn't *think* there was a mistake—no, no, I was sure there wasn't.

The defense attorney stretched his mustache across his face pleasantly, thanked me, and I was excused from the stand.

The defendant took the stand, his face a featureless, motionless mask. No, he didn't expose himself. Yes, he had served in the United States Army in Korea. Yes, he had a Purple Heart. Yes, he was a member of a reputable veterans' organization. Yes, he lived with his mother and supported her. Yes, he worked for the United States Post Office. No, he had never been arrested before. No, he did not expose himself, the girl was mistaken.

Since the defendant at a hearing is not cross-examined by the district attorney, Rettick was told to leave the stand.

The magistrate leaned forward to catch the attention of the court stenographer and mumbled something. "Case dismissed—reasonable doubt." And then the magistrate held his hand up to the stenographer, who nodded and kept his hands in his lap.

The magistrate motioned the defendant to the bench, and his attorney pushed his arm and brought him forward. The magistrate, a putty-faced man with gray temples and silver-streaked black hair spoke in a loud, clear voice, flinty with indignation.

"Young man, you keep away from schools and you keep away from young girls, and I don't ever want to see you in my court again, do you understand?"

The magistrate looked past the defendant, directly at me, and nodded, just once, almost imperceptibly. Yes, it had been for me.

The defendant stood mute and bewildered, not knowing if he was free to go or expected to say something—to protest his innocence or admit his guilt. His lawyer whispered something to him, and he muttered to the magistrate, or to the air, for he looked at space: "Yes. Thank you."

As he passed us, leaving the courtroom, Rettick stared at me for a moment, his colorless eyes searching my face as though he were trying to remember where he had seen me or to determine who I was. I sat rigidly watching him walk with his attorney out of the courtroom, and then Bayreuth stood up and we left the room without speaking.

The captain was outside, waiting for us. He was smiling and he waved.

"Fine," he said, "fine, Mrs. Uhnak. Would you like to have some lunch with me? My attorney is taking my brother home. We're going to make some arrangements, just as soon as possible, to get into the veterans' hospital." He held a hand against his flat stomach. "I'm really famished; let's get something to eat uptown, the places around here are ptomaine dens."

"No, thank you, Captain Rettick. I seem to have lost my appetite."

The captain stopped smiling, and his face became hard in a more natural setting of the thin cheek bones and square jaw and firm lips. "I told you this morning—and you'd better get it straight right now—forget this. *Just forget it.*"

And he walked away without looking back.

Bayreuth's face registered nothing, not sympathy or regret or indignation or anger. "You shouldn't have said anything. Look, Dot, it's just one of those things. It's just rough that it happened on your first pinch. It'll probably never happen again. It was a lousy case all around, so just like the man says: *forget it.*" His mouth pulled down and his hand pressed against his side—his ulcer.

I pretended I hadn't seen him holding his pain. "Sure, Bill, sure."

All the way home, in the subway, I thought all around the thing that was bothering me the most—not the case, not the way everything had been set up, not that. But the thing about myself: the hesitation on the stand, the accepting of a role, the acting out. And searching myself, trying to face it out, completely, honestly, I did not know if it had been deliberate hesitation or just due to my nervousness about being on a witness stand for the first time. Or was I avoiding it, trying to keep myself from the fact that I had been an integral part of it, trying to give myself an out? Did I have a choice? Could I have done anything about it? Had I just gone along with it, smoothly a part of it, so easily, so easily? I wasn't sure, not truly sure, but I knew I felt a nagging little knot of uncertainty and regret at having walked away from a senseless fight.

Four days later, assigned back to the Policewomen's Bureau, I picked up a telephone message from my mailbox. Mrs. Small wanted me to call immediately. It was very important.

Probably to tell me about the fine letter to the commissioner. Or maybe to explain why she hadn't written it after all. Perhaps Dr. Small felt it wouldn't be the proper thing to do. After all, they *did* pay my salary, wasn't that enough? Or maybe they wanted me to catch a rabid dog who had attacked their French poodle. Wasn't I paid for that kind of thing? One would assume so.

Mrs. Small's voice was edgier than it had been during our last conversation. Something was missing, possibly the social amenities. She sounded breathless. "Policewoman Uhnak, I'm so glad you called. I've been trying to reach you." She sounded slightly accusing, as though I'd been in hiding. "They told me at the precinct where you were."

"Yes, Mrs. Small. Look, I'm just on my way out on an assignment. I don't mean to be rude, but I'm in something of a hurry."

"I want to know what happened in court." There was an urgency and lack of composure in the voice of the doctor's wife.

"Nothing much, Mrs. Small." There was a savage pleasure in telling her this: a kind of revenge. "Nothing I couldn't have predicted."

"What do you mean?" She knew. *Now she knew.*

"The case was dismissed," I said matter of factly. It sounded so simple. "The magistrate felt there was a reasonable doubt: my word against the defendant's. He looked fairly presentable in court—shaved, combed, washed up. Not at all like a degenerate. Did you say something, Mrs. Small?"

She had gasped, and then she spoke very quickly, as though confiding a secret she could no longer contain. "Mrs. Uhnak, he's back again." She paused, waiting perhaps for me to reply to this incredible information, but I was silent. "He's back, I said. At the school. The girls have seen him. He . . . he *exposed himself* to the girls yesterday. They are absolutely terrified. Mrs. Uhnak, are you there? Did you hear me?"

Mrs. Small never would have understood my smile. There was something inside me, growing, growing. I was learning. All about it—the sincere statements, the outrage of the injured parties, and the golden assurances. I will take care of him, this won't happen again. You can be sure. You can be certain.

Of course he was back at the school; where else would he be? Of course he was out exposing himself; what else would he be doing? I was surprised at my lack of surprise. It was as though I had known all along that this phone call would come, even at the moment when Captain Rettick was telling us, earnestly and with great sincerity in his voice and eye, that his kid brother would be looked after, tended, treated, cured. Of course he was back. We had all arranged it; we were all a part of it. I was a part of it too, however unwilling an accessory. I knew that now, clearly, but I knew also that I had learned from it, that one more new lesson was etched into my mind.

"Mrs. Small, I'm sorry, but this isn't my concern. I suggest you call the precinct and speak with the desk officer. He'll assign someone to your complaint." And then, meanly, "You've been through all this before; you know the procedure."

For one crazy moment, it flashed through my mind to give Mrs. Small the telephone number of Captain Rettick. I tried to visualize the meeting of those two. But I didn't, of course, because the "good friend" would be an even worse enemy, and I knew my name would be carefully written down in a guarded little book somewhere.

Mrs. Small's voice penetrated my thoughts, and it was shrill with a kind of hopeless outrage. "But you must help us! You must arrest him!"

Ask Dr. Small what to do, lady. "No, ma'am," I said pleasantly, savoring the moment, "I already have. And Mrs. Small, about that letter you and the doctor were going to write to the commissioner—don't bother. I don't need it. You see, I have a very valuable friend and I don't need your letter of commendation."

I hung up the receiver before I heard Mrs. Small's reply.

5

"I have killed the child, and he was flesh of my flesh"

Periodically, as a policewoman, you have to handle what I consider the rottenest job possible: you put in time on what is called "D.O.A. reserve." You sit in the Policewomen's Bureau throughout your tour, awaiting a summons that will take you anywhere in the city where a dead female lies. In the presence of other police officers, you search the dead body and remove any jewelry or any other items that might be secreted on the body. These articles are tagged, enveloped and filed away until such time as relatives make a legitimate claim. This is a legal necessity whenever someone dies outside of a hospital and unattended by a physician.

In the two weeks I had been on D.O.A. reserve, I had been called on to search two dead women: old women, both of whom had died in their sleep of natural causes. One had been a spinster, a retired saleslady with long, slender, white fingers delicately etched with blue veins. She had lain neatly in a sparkling white bed, covered delicately to her chin with a soft white coverlet sprinkled with pink and green rosebuds. She was as barren of any jewelry as her room was barren of any dirt, any signs of decay. It was apparent that she had been a meticulous woman. Her hair was sparkling silver and well groomed, a trace of pale lipstick was on her lips. I had never seen a dead body before, and looking at her face, sleeping, in repose with a lasting dignity, I forced my mind into some blank emptiness, carefully running my hands over her limbs almost as though afraid to disturb her rest. There was an eloquent silence in the room except for the occasional sounds of the uniformed patrolman and the soft murmurings of the maid who had found her. No tears, no weeping for this dead stranger, and whatever life she had lived had died quietly and completely, without leaving a trace.

The second D.O.A. was a fat, wrinkled old woman who had been snatched into death secretly. Her family had gathered, waiting, waiting the long days and nights for her departure. The priest had come and gone and come again, but the old woman had held on fiercely, accepting the injections the doctor gave her with a tough determination, refusing to be sent to a hospital. The family had left for their various homes after the old woman had rallied loudly and demanded an end to their deathwatch. The old woman had fought death venomously, refusing to sleep, to close her eyes. One daughter had remained, finally, and had dozed and nodded at the old woman's bedside and had not heard the deep and triumphant death rattle seize the woman by the throat and throttle her into submission. The daughter panicked on awakening, unable to believe that the tough old woman had finally gone; she began screaming loudly, rushed to the telephone, forgot her brother's number and asked the operator for the police.

By the time we arrived, the small apartment was crowded with anguished women and sobbing men and openmouthed children in various stages of grief and excitement. One of the daughters-in-law pushed her husband's arm as I entered the room.

"Who's she?" she demanded.

The sergeant, hearing, explained. "A policewoman, ma'am. She has to search the body."

The woman seemed enraged. "Search the body? For what?"

Her husband tried to quiet her, but she narrowed her bitter gray eyes. "I want to see her search the body. She wears jewelry. I want to be there."

I turned away from the woman, catching the sergeant's hard grimace, and entered the small, cluttered room where the old woman's body lay. I noticed the stubby fingers: the nails were caked with some black substance. The woman wore a narrow gold wedding band on her left hand and a large, yellowish diamond ring on her right hand. The patrolman stood next to me and held up a small cloth bag.

"Take the rings off, put them in here." And then, kindly, "Is this your first?"

My fingers were trembling and my mouth was very dry. "No, second. But, well, the first one didn't have any jewelry. I didn't really have to do anything."

"Don't worry about it, just get a good grip on the rings, forget about everything but the rings." And then, in answer to my silent plea, he nodded toward the other room. "I'd do it for you, kid, but the sergeant's a real stickler." He whispered words of encouragement. "The fingers won't hurt you, girlie. Just get a good grip and pull."

The daughter-in-law standing on the other side of the bed could hear the sounds but not the words. She raised her face, suspiciously. "What are you whispering about? What are you doing with those rings? Why is she taking them off?"

The patrolman sighed patiently. "Regulations, ma'am. We'll put everything in this bag, and you or your husband can check the items and sign for them and pick them up at headquarters."

The yellow diamond had a dirty, unpleasant, dull cast. Trying not to touch the hand, I grasped the ring between two fingers and tugged. The ring wouldn't budge. The flesh had swollen and the finger claimed the ring for its own: the tough old lady wasn't giving up without a fight. I tried again but it wouldn't slide. I could hear the sergeant's voice in the other room, could feel the daughter-in-law watching closely. Taking a deep breath, I closed my eyes and grasped the dead hand with my own left hand, trying not to think, and yanked as hard as I could and it finally came free. I dropped the stiff hand back onto the bed. A shiver jerked my spine, then went up between my shoulder blades. I pulled the covers down quickly and looked at the terrible feet, sticking up with thick yellow toenails.

"No ankle bracelets," I said stiffly.

The patrolman smiled. He looked so old to be a cop.

I wondered why he hadn't retired about twenty years ago. He had an ancient face, but a kind expression. "Did you really think there would be?"

The daughter-in-law had to tend to a runny-nosed little boy who gaped, wide-eyed, at his dead grandmother, then threw himself on the floor and howled. She had to heave him to his heavy feet and drag him out of the room.

I began to feel giddy from the heat of the room and the noise of the mourners and that big lump of a woman lying on the bed, so fierce and resentful, as if she were going to sit up at any minute and bellow. Her jaw had stiffened and her upper lip had curled, revealing dirty teeth. I couldn't stop looking at her, but my hands wouldn't reach out any more. "That's it," I said, and we took the bag with the two rings to the outer room. The daughter-in-law left her son sitting on a chair snuffling and pushed aside two sisters to examine the rings. The sisters did not look at the bag, but looked up, wet-faced and in surprise when their sister-in-law suddenly began shouting.

"Wait a minute, just you wait a minute! Where are her bracelets? What have you done with her bracelets?"

The sergeant looked up, and everyone in the room seemed to be staring at me, even the messy little boy. The woman was furious and her voice was shrill. "Don't try to fool around with me. I know you people! You police! She always wore her bracelets." She pushed her husband's hand off her arm. "You remember, the gold bracelet with the diamond and the one with the ruby. She always said I could have them. Where are they? Where the hell are they?"

"Monica," her husband pleaded, "come on now, shut up, please. Have some respect. Mama's in there dead."

"Yeah, she's dead and I want to know where her bracelets are! Who do I see around here?" And to the sergeant, "You! You're their boss or something, huh? My mother-in-law always wore bracelets, she even slept with them. They are very valuable. Where are they?"

The sergeant's face was ruddy, and slowly the flushing

of blood boiled through his heavy cheeks. He turned from the woman with great effort and asked me, "Any bracelets, officer?"

I could feel the pounding at my temples and the cold moisture running down my arms. I hadn't searched the woman's arms under the gray nightgown. "I didn't see any, sarge."

Very quietly, he said, "Let's go inside and take another look."

The dead woman's wrists, freckled and stained with age, were sticking out of the crumpled sleeves of her flannel nightgown. The sergeant ran his hands quickly up the woman's arms to the shoulder, then stiffened and turned, red-faced, to me.

His voice was high-pitched, surprising in such a big man. "Did you check her arms? Did you run your hands up her arms?"

"No, sergeant."

"Well, do it now," he said tersely.

The bracelets were high above the woman's elbows: two narrow brownish-gold bangles, one with a rusty diamond chip, the other with a dull red ruby chip. I pulled them off the woman's arms, desperately bunching the dead fingers together in order to free the bracelets from her hands.

The daughter-in-law scowled. "I understand how they work it now. When they got Mama downtown, they'd divide the bracelets. I'm gonna report them. Don't tell me to shush, Frank. I knew what they were up to!"

I think it was because of his resentment of the daughter-in-law that the sergeant didn't give me an official reprimand. He should have, of course, and back at the precinct I listened wordlessly to his abusive lecture, agreeing with him, nodding, the humiliation burning my cheeks. His anger, however, was diverted when he thought of the daughter-in-law, and he ended with a severe warning. We could all have been in serious trouble had the woman made an official complaint, but the son had assured the sergeant that his wife was upset—with grief—and that he would not let her go any further in the matter. The daughter-in-law, at any rate, had seemed placated once she held the treasured bracelets in her hands.

I was determined, on my third call, that I would be thorough. All the way to the address, on the Lower East Side, the patrolman assigned as the D.O.A. driver regaled me endlessly with stories about the various bloody, headless, armless corpses that he had searched; about the bloated look of drowned people and the mess of subway suicides and the gore of jumpers. Whether he did this to show me that all of this was just natural and that one had to adopt a casual attitude toward dead people or to reassure me that my next D.O.A. couldn't possibly compare to his own messy storehouse of memories, I didn't know. I only wished he would shut up—and take a bath occasionally. He smelled terrible.

The address was of a tenement on a street of tenements and garbage-laden lots. I walked up the four flights of stairs, trying not to breathe the inevitable smell of ancient, rotting, narrow hallways and wooden staircases. I could feel the dampness and heaviness folding around my body as though I had stepped into a shower of steam and filth.

The neighbors were standing at each landing, looking upward, talking in excited tones, pushing each other's bodies with their elbows as I passed. They noted my blue uniform and drew back slightly to let me pass in a gesture of respect, yet at the same time of contempt for the official, the outsider.

I avoided their eyes, their faces, but was aware of their bodies: large, sweaty, heavy with rich and ugly odors. The door of one of the three flats on the top floor was flung open, and I could hear the rumble of masculine conversation. I tried to breathe shallowly, not wanting to fill myself with this breathless air, yet I felt a desperate need to fill my lungs. When I entered the room lit with bare yellow bulbs, the patrolman glanced up, nodded at me, then continued with his work, jotting notes in his memo book.

A large, dark-haired man with heavy black brows turned from where he was bending under the sink and nodded at me. "I'm Lieutenant Storenoff," he said.

"Yes, sir. Policewoman Uhnak, from D.O.A. reserve."

His voice was low and growling. "D.O.A. reserve?" His brows shot up at the patrolman.

"Gee, Lieutenant, I called the Bureau. This is what they sent me."

They both regarded me, and I had a vague, passing hope that I was sent in error and they were going to send me back.

The lieutenant finally grunted, "Doesn't matter." Then he jerked his head toward the curtained doorway leading to the next room. "We've got a woman in there," he said.

I started for the room, but he said, "No, wait a minute. Sit down for a minute."

He continued making some notations in his book and I looked around for a place to sit. That was a homicide car we had seen parked outside the building; what was waiting for me in the next room?

Concentrating on the room I was in, I tried to fix it in my mind, to find some cohesiveness in the conglomeration of items. The walls were a faded pink, the molding was outlined in pale blue. In the middle of the room was a small, battered kitchen table. An overstuffed chair in one corner was covered with a reddish material, with thick vines creeping up its sides and around the cushion. The windows were covered with long, stiff curtains made from strips of bright material sewn together crazily without thought to pattern or design. Between the two long narrow windows there was a picture of a sad and sallow-faced Virgin holding a fat, flaccid child against her shoulder. She was staring at the child with slightly crossed blue eyes, and the child was grinning vacantly. There was a small stove and refrigerator against the wall opposite the windows, next to a scarred sink, and the water dripped. Underneath the sink was a dirty army blanket, and next to the army blanket was a chair. I sat down on the edge of it.

"Hey, don't sit there!" the lieutenant said, turning to me. "Jesus, you've got your foot on him!"

I leaped to my feet. "On who?"

The lieutenant closed his notebook and jammed it into

a back pocket. He bent over heavily, for he was a large man, not fat, but big, and he pulled the blanket back.

"Here," he said. "The kid. Take a look."

There was a small, crumpled body under the sink lying half on its side, its face lying in a thick pool of its own blood. There were great open gashes about the head and face and long swollen red welts on the bare white arms and legs. One fat white hand was pressed down flat, and under the hand was a kind of rag doll. The fingernails of the hand were gnawed down almost to the roots: dried blood lined each nail. For some reason I could not take my eyes off the chewed nails. I felt a cry coming from somewhere deeper inside of me than seemed possible and I clenched my teeth to hold it in, to force it back, but a small sigh like the catching of breath escaped and I nearly gagged on the force of the cry that was rushing against my throat.

"Nice, huh?" the lieutenant said, and he tossed the cover over the body.

"What happened?" I didn't recognize my own voice.

"There's an old woman in there. Come here. Look at her."

He held aside the long curtain and I looked into the next room and saw an old woman, round and small and dressed in black, sitting and rocking on the edge of a high bed, her misshapen shoes skimming the floor. She was moaning softly, clutching her body, her long, yellowed gray hair falling across her face.

Lieutenant Storenoff let the curtain drop back into place. "She's the grandmother. She says that some strange big man, some big black man came in and beat the kid to death. With that broom," he pointed across the room and my eyes followed his finger, "and that frying pan. Some stranger, she says."

His voice was oddly flat and soft, without expression, and he recited the words in some incredibly rational way. I searched his tiny black eyes to see if he really believed this: he said it so calmly. But his face revealed nothing. A large square face with dark stubble on the cheeks and huge jaws and heavy lips, and those terrible dark little eyes. I had heard about homicide men: his face was a mask.

"Some stranger?" I asked in bewilderment. "But why? Why would any stranger . . ."

I stopped speaking, for he blinked at me in an expression of cold contempt. "We requested a policewoman from the Bureau; there must have been some cross-up and they sent you from reserve. But as long as you're here, you'll do," he said, making the best of a poor bargain. Then, to the patrolman, "Keep an eye on Grandma. We're going to visit some of the neighbors." He motioned to me to follow and did not look at me again.

They were eager to talk, the neighbors, nodding their heads and inviting us into their homes. Three of the women came into one of the flats, while their husbands stood leaning against various doorways. One was sitting on the edge of the sink one flight directly below the place where the boy's body lay. The woman offered coffee, which the lieutenant accepted and I refused. I was afraid of choking on the air and the liquid and the sounds of their voices.

This old woman, they told us, this Angelina Bacardi, had had a terrible life. A sad and terrible and thankless life, and she such a good old woman. Fervently crossing themselves with their rough, reddened hands, rolling their eyes to the cracked, chipping ceiling and intoning the name of the Virgin, they told, speaking in relays, how Angelina Bacardi had been the mother of six good children, and then had given birth to *that one:* Annamarie, with the thick black curls and flashing eyes. This little one, she had been her father's favorite. Old Guido cherished her, adored her, worshiped her, this child of their old age. But it was wrong and turned out badly.

The three women exchanged glances, nodded at each other, clucked their tongues in growing excitement. I noticed one of the husbands, a small, hard, muscular man, leaning against the sink. I watched as he moved the tip of his shoe, digging it into a small hole in the linoleum; his face had stiffened and he seemed to be exerting great pressure with his foot.

"The boy," the lieutenant asked quietly, "who was the boy?"

That started again the flow of scornful words with the strange undertones I could not quite identify.

That Annamarie, that beautiful angel, they said. When she was fifteen, everyone in the neighborhood knew what she was, that cheap little thing. Everyone but Guido, because he didn't want to know, but he had to know sooner or later. That is the one thing you cannot hide. She had the child, the Devil's child, and she didn't even know who the father was. How could she have known: no one knew, it could have been any one of ten or more. Yes, any one of fifty.

The man near the sink glanced quickly at another of the husbands, who was sitting on the edge of the window sill: a dark-faced man with thick curly hair, who lifted his chin slightly and squinted his eyes and ran his tongue along his full lower lip. The man near the sink looked down again at his feet, then looked up, directly into my eyes. His cheeks seemed to darken and he dropped his eyes.

I thought of the beautiful Annamarie as they hissed the words of their story: fifteen years old and slender with black curls and flashing eyes. I saw these strong and masculine and lusty men, sitting here in this room with their women, these youthless young women in their late thirties or early forties who had no shining thing about them. I looked at the third husband, who was leaning against the doorjamb, lighting a new cigarette from the stub of his old one, a strong man, as the other two were strong, with work-blackened hands and a hard mouth.

"And the boy?" the lieutenant asked.

She had the boy, this little angel, and it killed Guido, really killed him, for the boy was born right upstairs. One Tuesday, the boy was born, and two days later—it was six, yes, six years ago—on a Thursday, Guido died of heartbreak. And the old woman, in her grief and shame, sent the girl out the day her father died.

I spoke so unexpectedly that even I was surprised. "Sent the girl out? Sent her out where?"

The woman who had been speaking turned a hard, shrewd face toward me, then shrugged her shoulders and spread her hands. "Out. Out to the street, where she belonged!"

Lieutenant Storenoff's little eyes were fixed on my face. Without saying a word or changing his stony expression, he warned me; I pressed my lips together and said nothing.

"And the child?" he prompted softly.

Ah, the child was evil and bad; from the beginning the child had been cursed. The Dumb One, they called him: he never spoke a word. His head was large but not with brains, and wobbly, and dropped from side to side. And he never had a name, not that they knew of, just the Dumb One, for that was what he was.

I wondered which of the women were married to which of the men, tried to match them up, pair them off. But they looked incredibly alike: shapeless and gray with heavy, unwashed hair pulled back behind their ears with bobby pins: large, strong, meaningless faces that seemed to blur without expression; stubby strong hands, rough and red as men's hands. I knew they had been studying me; I had felt the cold, hate-filled glances exchanged between them and I tried to breathe steadily and slowly, to control the rhythmic, sudden waves of despair that rushed through my body like blood. They were some ancient race of women who feed on damnation and ruin of the young and the beautiful, who wet their lips and teeth over the destruction of beauty, and nod and cross themselves and crack their knuckles and squint their eyes in pleasure, as though in some long-awaited revenge and justification. And their men were present with them, but not of them. No man looked at his woman when she spoke, no eyes were meeting, no feeling shared. They were separate and apart and not of each other. I knew what the strange hidden tones in their voices were as they related the tragedy to us: some terrible dull kind of joy and triumph. They had prevailed. The beautiful Annamarie was vanquished and the devil-child was dead.

When one stopped speaking another began, but it was the same voice telling the story with the same insistent monotonous tone. He would not learn, that one. She tried to teach him, the poor old woman, burdened now with this one in her old age. Sixty-four and raised six good children, and all gone away now and married. This was her gift in her old age, this one that slobbered and moaned and howled all night. But she tried, the Virgin is her witness, she tried. She was not a strong woman, always with the pains in her shoulders, and why not, dragging that great fat one up the four steep flights of stairs day after day. Taking him to the playground, putting him with the children so that he might learn to play. But the children hit him and threw him to the ground and spat upon him, and the old woman would pull him up and make him stand, and tell him to hit back, and punch him, to show him. But he would lie down and howl and ruin his clothing, the stupid one.

I lifted my head, felt words in my mouth, but Lieutenant Storenoff stopped me cold, as though anticipating me, and I said nothing, holding this thing down inside of me, forcing it back and down. I felt a terrible, growing, aching pain, and then an urgent, dreadful need to run from this room, this building, this world of theirs to the night streets, to any place where the air was cold and pure, away from these death-chanters.

No, she could not leave the Dumb One alone—not for a minute. Always, he had to be with her. One time, she had tried to leave him, so that she could visit some friends. She had tied him with a long rope to the bed, so that he could move around but not get out, not get into trouble. But somehow he had broken the rope—he was very strong—and he had gotten into the front room and found the matches and set fire to the curtains, and the husband of one of the women had rushed up the stairs and put out the fire, or they all would have died.

The woman sitting directly across from me turned and nodded vigorously toward the man leaning against the sink, and he looked at the ceiling, nodding only slightly, and made a clicking sound with his tongue against his front teeth and dug his shoe into the floor.

And when the old woman came home, later that night,

she cried and screamed, she was so upset. The curtains were all black, and there was water all over the front room. She screamed and the Dumb One moaned, and the old woman took a match and lit it and held it to his palm to try to teach him. To try to teach him. Then she handed the stupid one the matches, and didn't he try to light one? They had all taught their own children this way, and their own children would never touch matches.

Ignoring the lieutenant, who had focused his gaze on me, I asked: "You burned your children's hands?"

The women stopped speaking, pulled the sleeves of their heavy sweaters and blinked vacantly, and there was a heavy, resentful silence in the small yellowish room.

"And tonight," the lieutenant asked, "what happened tonight?"

Their narrative had been broken; they shrugged heavily, staring at their hands. The lieutenant sighed, then took out a long cigar and motioned with it toward his mouth for permission. The woman whose home it was nodded and got up and brought him an ash tray. The man by the sink reached into a cupboard over his head and brought out an unmarked bottle of wine.

Would the lieutenant like some homemade wine? The lieutenant had a small glass of homemade wine, and the man gave me some of the deep red liquid in a small, dirty juice glass. His fingers touched mine as he handed me the glass; his eyes were like glittering beads, sliding down my face and down the length of my body to my legs and ankles and back to my knees. He stood against the sink again, drinking a water glass of the wine, surveying me openly with an amused expression, for his wife's back was to him.

"And tonight," the lieutenant said, "the boy upset her tonight?"

Ah, tonight, last night, a thousand nights for six years of nights the boy had upset her: this devil with the stubborn body that could feel nothing, but could eat the food and outgrow the clothes the old woman had to sew for him.

Tonight, yes. He spilled the coffee.

"Spilled the coffee?"

The woman ignored me and spoke only to the lieutenant. It was the old woman's only pleasure, the coffee. And she shared it with *that one*. She made a fresh pot every morning, and they drank it for breakfast and lunch and then at night. The boy had been bad that day, as always. Not watching where he walked, falling into the gutter and cutting his hand and ripping his sleeve, not caring. It never hurt him. He had no feelings. And then he had fallen down the stairs and pulled the old woman with him, and all of her packages had fallen. The boy had sat on the steps instead of helping her to pick the things up. He had sat down and pushed his fingers into the eggs and laughed, and the old woman had had to climb down the stairs and pick up the things. And then, when they got inside, he had begun to scream, and there had been much noise and he had spilled the coffee.

"How do you know he spilled the coffee?" the lieutenant asked.

Everyone knew: you could hear. The old woman had a very loud voice, and it had been a bad day for her. She screamed it over and over again, as though she couldn't stop the words from coming from her lips. Over and over again she screamed that he had spilled the coffee.

"And then what happened?" he asked.

And the women rolled their eyes and shrugged and crossed themselves. What happened then? Why, who would know? There was much screaming and much noise and much terrible sound. And then it was quiet.

And then it was quiet.

"And then what happened?" the lieutenant asked in a quiet chanting way, as children ask the storyteller.

And then the old woman had knocked on a neighbor's door.

The woman sitting on the edge of the upholstered chair nodded and glanced at the man standing against the doorjamb.

And the neighbor and her husband went upstairs with the old woman. And then they called the police. And that was all.

And that was all.

There was an inaudible general sigh in the room from the three women. There it was, all told, and that was all, and their lips were shut now and their eyebrows were raised expectantly.

I didn't hear the lieutenant's words, just the soft, even hum of his voice. I stood up because I realized that he was leaving, and I turned for some reason before I left the flat. The man leaning against the sink grinned and winked, behind his wife's back, and made an obscene gesture at me with his hands.

When we entered the old woman's flat, I did not sit down but stared at the floor near where the army blanket lay, and noticed for the first time the dark, still damp stain of the spilled coffee.

Lieutenant Storenoff had his back to me and I didn't hear him, but apparently he had said something, for he turned facing me, looking down at me, his face still and blank.

"I said, go in there and search the prisoner."

I rubbed my hands together convulsively, trying to find something to hold onto. "I can't. I'm sorry, lieutenant, but I'm going to be sick."

I could feel the blood draining from my face and the cold lightheaded sickness and the beads of perspiration on my mouth and cheeks. His voice was an odd mixture of anger and softness, and he suddenly grasped my arm with his powerful hand and pulled me toward the sink. He bent over, still holding my arm, and pulled the blanket back from the child's body, then released my arm and straightened up.

"Listen," he said. "Listen, this is a corpse. Dead. Without feeling or anything else, just a dead thing. Whether it was six years old or seventy or hacked to death or beaten to death or poisoned or died of natural causes, right now it is absolutely nothing. This is when we get it: when it doesn't matter any more."

I stared at the side of the child's face, the heavy cheek lying in the thick blood, and then at the bitten, ragged nails of the child who felt nothing, had not experienced pain, was too stupid. The lieutenant drew back his foot and kicked the body roughly, and I felt a cry and stared at him in horror.

"It's nothing," he said, his eyes not blinking. "Now, I don't know how long you've been a cop or how long you intend to stay one, but the Bureau sent you over here and your job now is to go in and search that female prisoner. Go and be sick if you have to, and then when you're finished, go and search her."

I could not get the sickness from my stomach. It was down too far, in my legs, and rising into my chest. I pressed my shoulder as hard as I could against the corrugated tin wall of the narrow closetlike enclosure where the toilet was, saw an ancient calendar on the wall, decorated with yellow roses.

I dug my nails into the palms of my hands, needing to feel something, some distinct, actual, real pain, some sign of my own existence. When I left the cubicle, Lieutenant Storenoff turned to me and said softly, "Listen, Miss . . . What's your first name?" I told him. "Listen, Dorothy. When you leave here tonight, it's all over. Finished. You leave and you forget it."

I nodded, but I knew he was wrong. It was what they all were telling me: you forget it. But I had felt the insistent little pieces of memory pushing inside of me all night. The sensations and special combination of odors, the tone of voice, the inflections, the gestures, the special haze of yellow light. I knew they were stored, unrelated, in some compartment of my brain. I knew that all my life they would appear before me, unexpectedly, in different places, at different times, and would conjure up this house, this world, these people. He was wrong, but I knew that the words had cost him something, and so I nodded and entered the bedroom.

The old woman stared up dumbly at me as I motioned for her to rise. I avoided the old woman's face and quickly ran my hands under her clothing. The woman had nothing on her body but her age: all the days and nights

and years of her life, filling her with a musty, stale and
deathly odor.

"A big black man, miss, he beata the boy. He beata
the boy, God help him."

The woman sat down on the bed again, rocking her
body back and forth, her feet dangling two inches from
the floor. Seeing those two feet, swollen and hanging in
space, apart and separate from the terribleness of the
woman, I felt I did not want to see them, did not want
to feel the senseless, irrational pity the sight of those
old feet drew forth. I wanted to see the strong old hands
that could beat a helpless, demented child to death, not
the tired, misshapen, old and helpless feet of an old woman who had borne seven children and was now here,
alone, holding her ancient body and moaning and praying
in some monotonous liturgy to her ideal of all motherhood.
I looked at the woman's face, wanting to despise her,
needing to despise her, looked for the signs of loathsome-
ness. Instead I saw an old and creased and ignorant face,
blackened with time and sunken with rotten teeth, twitching in prayer and bewilderment. The colorless eyes were
swimming in tears which cut jagged paths down the sallow
cheeks. I went back to the front room and said to the
lieutenant: "Nothing. Nothing on her."

He nodded and turned to a slim, dark-haired man who
had just arrived. "This is Detective Navarra. Get the old
woman in here."

I approached the woman and touched her shoulder
lightly with my hand, not looking at her, and made a
gesture toward the front room. The old woman got to the
floor and hobbled into the front room, and the Italian-
speaking detective pulled out a chair for her. She sat down
heavily.

"Now, tell us, Mama; no one here will hurt you. Tell
us what happened here tonight."

The old woman, hearing the soft-voiced words of her
own language, looked at the detective and then around
the room, and then at the Virgin with the fat child in her
arms. Then she shrieked, her voice the ripping, tearing,

cutting sound of an animal in desperate pain. Over and over she shrieked some words, holding her body in her arms and beseeching the slightly cross-eyed Virgin.

Lieutenant Storenoff stood unblinking, unmoving, watching the woman. Suddenly, the screaming stopped and with a wordless gasp the old woman threw herself to the floor and crept under the sink and pulled the blanket back and began petting and kissing the dead child. When they pulled her back onto the chair, she was holding on to the dirty piece of rag, shaped vaguely like a doll, which she had taken from the dead child's hand. She petted and caressed the doll with a hand wet with blood.

"What did she say?" Lieutenant Storenoff asked.

The Italian-speaking detective took a deep breath and his voice seemed shaky. "She said: 'I have killed the child, and he was flesh of my flesh.'"

Lieutenant Storenoff blinked once, his eyes closing completely, like a cat or an owl, but he did not move or nod. Then, opening his eyes, he motioned to me. "All right, officer, you and the patrolman take her to the precinct. Detective Navarra, you go, too. The M.E. will be here in a few minutes, and I'll be down within an hour. And, Miss Uhnak, I phoned your office, so you're covered."

I touched the woman's arm, my fingers trembling at the narrowness of the bones beneath the grayish-black eternal mourning sleeve of her dress. The old woman looked up at me, startled, then at Navarra, who told her in Italian to come and not be frightened.

As we reached the door, Lieutenant Storenoff called out sharply, his voice louder and harsher than I had heard it. "Wait a minute," he said. Then he walked to us, and without a word he wrenched the small piece of rag from the woman's hand. The woman recoiled with a short cry of terror or anguish, and her arms reached out and her body shuddered; I held her, or she would have sunk to the floor.

Lieutenant Storenoff, without looking at us, walked to the sink and pulled the blanket back, placed the rag doll under the child's hand and recovered the body carefully. Then he turned to us.

He stood scowling for a second, looking directly at me. Then his features rearranged themselves; he adjusted the mask of blankness and lifted an arm at us. "Go ahead," he said softly. "Get going."

6

"A terrible thing was done to me"

There is a rhythm and a cadence to police work. There are long slow weeks when the eight-hour tour seems empty beyond endurance, when you hear about other people's excitements and accomplishments and encounters, and you have the feeling that you are plodding through mud, that whatever it was you were supposed to learn, to do, to partake of, is lost and gone, not to happen. Then, it changes. Something happens, some investigation, some arrest, and the tempo picks up with lightning speed. It always seems to happen in cycles—you make one arrest and you get hot, and one seems to follow the other.

In the long routine stretches between the activity, the faces of people become a blur, their voices a low and monotonous moan of complaints. This was done to me. Where were the police? I was never so shocked, I was never so outraged, I was never so frightened. And you look at the people and listen to their stories and take down their words and turn them into the dry, official investigation reports that state the who-what-where-when. You learn to listen to the words without any sense of surprise. This thing has happened before, and as the inspector had told us, this thing will happen again. Soon none of the stories are new, so quickly have they become familiar and recognizable.

You have entree into an amazing number of homes and partake, fleetingly, of an amazing number of lives. You become a confidante on short acquaintance. They reveal things to you, at times unaware, giving themselves away with gestures or inflections. You never comment, you listen and you weigh and you evaluate and you learn to become accurate in your judgments. Though they had said you were not to judge, that you were only to gather the facts, the evidence, you learn instinctively to be suspicious of the blatantly stated words. You seek what is behind the words, and you find yourself taking nothing, *nothing,* at face value.

I shifted around, through the months, from the Policewomen's Bureau to the various precincts and squads where they needed a policewoman for a particular assignment. I learned to look at the various boroughs, to define the neighborhoods, to get the feel of the generations that had created islands within the city—distinct cultures with separate standards.

I was assigned to accompany a Brooklyn detective one morning, on an 8 to 4, to interview a complainant relative to an alleged rape the previous evening. All crimes reported are recorded as "alleged" until the facts are clear and the truth of the matter is known. Things you had accepted at face value a few brief months ago widen out, expand, take different shapes and meanings; you begin to pick out the questions, you become convinced that every complaint is an "alleged" incident, and you arrive for the interview without any certainties and many doubts. If your attitude seems offensive, you are sorry and try to keep your voice even, your doubts covered, to be the good listener.

Detective Frank Warener was a short, stocky man with traces of a rough black beard and deep-set, small, warm brown eyes. He had a quick smile and a deep voice and a calm and easy manner. His stubby strong hands, with a dangerous signet ring, waved around over the steering wheel of his car as he drove us to the neighborhood in Brooklyn where the complainant lived. He was warm and friendly and of that category of policemen who make just one slight distinction when assigned to work with a woman: they watch the casual interjection of four-letter words, catch their tongue between their teeth and insert an innocuous expression in place of profanity. He talked about a case he had been on, not bragging, chuckling over an amusing sidelight. In short, in speaking to me, he was speaking to a fellow worker, without resentment and in a common language. I had worked with women partners who were rougher in speech and men partners who were purposely crude, and I knew that Frank Warener and I were in communication and that he would lead the interrogation but I would be a party to it.

The house was a solid-looking brick with a flagstone patio, and was flanked on either side by similar but not quite identical houses. The street was tree-shaded. There was a kind of upper-middle-class solidity that seemed far removed from the comic implications generally associated with the borough's name. This was a part of Brooklyn I had never seen before, nor even knew existed. It was a kind of isolated, insulated, faintly disdainful little section, fringed on all sides by old wooden structures with porches and sad, fading gentility. When Frank pushed the doorbell, we heard a four-note lilting tune, clear and full. Then a light filled the small triangle of stained glass, and we heard a muffled sound and saw the door open a few inches, stopped short by a chain from within.

"Yes," the woman said, "who is it, please?"

Frank held his shield in the palm of his hand and raised it toward the voice.

"Detective Warener, and this is Policewoman Uhnak, ma'am. I called you about an hour ago."

"Yes, yes, I see. Just a moment, please." The door closed and there was a metallic clinking and then it opened again, wide. "Won't you come in, please?"

She was a fairly tall woman and was wearing some kind of wrapper and furry pink slippers. She led us into the living room, an attractive, well-furnished room with pale walls and carpeting, closed from the daylight by heavy, expensive draperies. The woman nodded at us and held her hands toward the couch. We sank into the soft, downy cushions. The room had a very high ceiling, with four massive dark beams; there was a wide, high fireplace set in one wall, and a tremendous abstract painting over the fireplace dominated the room. It was blazing with great slashes of pure color: reds fired into yellows and blues with areas of white darting in and out toward the edges.

It caught the eye immediately, and the woman, noticing me studying it, followed my eyes.

"It's exciting, isn't it?" she asked. "A young friend of mine, a young man named Miguel Hernández, did it for me. It seems new every time I look at it."

I didn't like the painting: there was something violent and furious about the slashes and stabs of color, something uncontrolled.

"It's very interesting," I said carefully.

Frank regarded the picture briefly, squinting, then cleared his throat. "Mrs. Crimmons, we'd like to ask you about what happened last night. I know you've spoken to the detectives already, but we've been assigned to the case, and we'd like to get the story firsthand."

The woman was sitting in a chair covered with some gold, shiny material. The wrapper she wore was iridescent and kept changing from red to green with each flicker of movement. She leaned back into the form of the chair and seemed to get smaller, to be holding herself tightly together, to seek some protection and some identity from the limits of the chair.

"Yes, yes," she said, her voice now softer, thicker. "A terrible thing was done to me. A terrible thing."

Instinctively, the words now were mine. "We understand that, Mrs. Crimmons. We know it's very difficult for you, but we must ask you to tell us about it."

"Of course," said Mrs. Crimmons. "I realize that. You've all been so nice, you police officers. Can I get you anything—coffee, a drink?"

She made vague, tentative gestures with her hands, apparently toward the kitchen, but she did not rise, and we both shook our heads. "Well, then, I shall tell you about it. I'm not a hysterical woman, but it isn't pleasant, as I'm sure you'll agree."

We nodded our agreement.

"Well," she began, "I live alone. As you can see," her right arm swept the room, "I have this large house and, of course, I do have help. So even with this large house, there isn't too much for me to do. Mr. Crimmons, my late husband, provided very nicely for me. He bought this house in my name six years ago, when we were married. He died last year, you know. Heart. I always told him he went at things too hard. I lost my first husband that way, and he was a young man, but you can't tell men anything, can you?"

She smiled sadly and shrugged, as though at the foolishness of men. "And though I do have my friends, of course, it does get a bit tiresome, lonely even, and I have always tried to keep interested in things. I'm not a woman to play cards or things like that. I like creative things—to keep active. To keep—young." She flashed a warm, broad smile. "Well, all this is beside the point, of course. I am greatly interested in art, and I learned of a very fine artist. Ricardo Domingo—you've heard of him? Well, at any rate, he is quite well known, and he lives just fifteen minutes from here. He was offering instruction, limited, of course, to those who met his specifications." She laughed, disparaging her own admittance to this select group. "I did a little sketching in my youth—I fancied myself an artist in those days." She sighed, a little weary, a little reminiscent. "But my first husband objected," she spread her palms upward, "so of course I gave it up. When he died, I was alone and didn't have funds to pick up my work again. Mr. Fredericks, God rest his soul, was a fine man, young and strong and very handsome, but not, well, not sensitive, if you know what I mean, and, poor boy, not a good provider. We lived on love, you might say." Mrs. Crimmons smiled fondly. "So I had to go to work, not exactly what my dear mother and father had had in mind for their only daughter. But then, I had run away from Miss Lighten's school to marry Mr. Fredericks, and I didn't dare to return home. I was a proud girl, you see. Well, at any rate, I went to work in one of the finest ladies' shops in Baltimore—that's where Mr. Fredericks and I had been living, you know. And then, the manager of the store, Mr. Donaldson—he was such a large man and so strong, and *seemed* such a fine man—well, we became acquainted and he quite swept me off my feet, and we were married within three months. Can you imagine the terrible situation—a widow of not quite four months. But then, I was only seventeen and not used to being alone."

I looked past Mrs. Crimmons to the painting again, tracing the dashes of red in and out of a maze of blues and yellows. I bit the corner of my lip hard, trying to revive myself from the warm, lilting quality of the woman's interminable words.

"Well," Mrs. Crimmons continued, ignoring Frank's raised hand, his attempt at interruption. Frank glanced at me, his eyes flickering, shrugging slightly. "Mr. Donaldson seemed such a fine man." Her eyes narrowed as she studied her fingers for a moment. "Until after we were married, that is. Unfortunately, we cannot learn these things before marriage—not a decent woman, at any rate. He was a fine big man and all of that, but he had an infirmity, you might say, which, well . . ." She stopped herself with a quick, sad smile at Frank. "We don't have to go into all of that now. Suffice to say he was not a man. Oh outwardly, of course, big and hearty and robust. But on our wedding night . . . Well, he was really a good man, you must understand, and I suppose he felt I might have helped him somehow with his 'problem.'" She pronounced the word delicately. "But I was really quite naïve about those things. At any rate, Mr. Donaldson was really quite kind, and he gave me an annulment and very kindly provided for me. I came to New York, where I lived for many years, until I met dear Mr. Crimmons, God rest his soul, and when we were married . . ."

I noticed a thin line of moisture on Frank's forehead, and his eyes had a kind of glazed look. He nodded his head from time to time as Mrs. Crimmons spoke directly to him.

"When we were married, Mr. Crimmons absolutely insisted I continue with my art work—he was so very proud of me." She laughed archly. "And I have dabbled now and again, but when he passed on—last year that was—I found that Mr. Domingo, a talented boy, a *talented* boy, was conducting courses. And practically in the neighborhood. Every Thursday evening from 7:30 to 10:30, and it seemed such a lovely opportunity."

The complete silence came so suddenly and so unexpectedly that Frank took a deep breath and then, trying to exhale, began to choke. Mrs. Crimmons leaned forward, expectantly, and Frank, red-faced, his voice strangling, asked her: "And you went last night? To the art class?"

"Yes, yes, last night was Thursday and I attended the class. And you must understand . . ."

Frank interrupted, almost desperately. "Where is Mr. Domingo located, Mrs. Crimmons?"

Mrs. Crimmons recited an address, which I jotted down, and before Frank could speak again, she had resumed. "And I worked on such a lovely drawing—a street scene from home. I'm from Georgia, you know. A lovely scene from my childhood which . . ."

Frank's eyes were popping and he shook his head and broke in. "Yes, of course, and what time did you leave Mr. Domingo's?"

"Oh, yes, I am getting wordy, I'm so very sorry, Detective Warener. I left there about 10:30—the usual time."

"And where did you go?"

"Where? Oh, of course. I generally take the bus home, but it was such a lovely night that . . ."

"Last night?" I was thinking of the rainy windstorm of the previous evening.

Mrs. Crimmons laughed, a soft, long sound. "You must think me mad, but I simply dote on wind and rain. There's something so refreshing, so cleansing. To me—forgive me —it was a lovely, wet, black night, and I decided to walk home, to feel the freshness on my face. I'd walked two blocks and turned down the avenue and was about halfway down the block. I was walking along, you understand, thinking about home—of that warm, dusty, yellow street with all that sunshine and . . ."

"Yes?" Frank said.

Mrs. Crimmons blinked, smiled and awoke from the reverie. "Yes. Well, at any rate, I passed this car, and this young man was sitting behind the wheel, you know, on the driver's side, and he poked his head out the window and called out something. I was startled, I hadn't noticed ım sitting there, and I turned and said, 'I beg your pardon?' He asked me the time, and I looked at my watch and told him it was twenty minutes to eleven. Yes, that's exactly right, twenty minutes to eleven, and then he began asking me directions and . . .''

"What directions did he ask you?"

Mrs. Crimmons shrugged a little impatiently at Frank. "My dear, I have no idea: some street, some street. I don't quite remember. And then he got out of the car, while I was speaking . . .''

"What were you saying?"

Mrs. Crimmons regarded me coldly and brushed away any response, continuing. "He came alongside of me, and then, forgive me if I tell all this rather quickly, then he was holding me around the throat and with a hand over my mouth he threw me into the car and came into the car beside me, and he said terrible things to me—that he had a knife and would cut my throat and other dreadful things and . . .''

"Did you see a knife? Did he show you a knife?" Frank asked quietly.

Mrs. Crimmons made a sharp clicking noise with her tongue and drew herself taller in the chair. "I didn't ask him to show me a weapon. I certainly believed he had a knife and that he was entirely capable of using it."

"Yes," Frank said softly. "And this was at twenty minutes to eleven?"

"Yes, and I was terrified, absolutely terrified, you cannot imagine my horror. I believed he was quite capable of murdering me. He drove the car away around streets and down avenues and I don't know where-all, and then he pulled into some big open place, behind some big buildings—they looked like factories or something. He must have known exactly where he was going because he drove directly there, you see, and then he pulled me from the car and forced me into the back seat. Then he came into the back seat, and then he did a terrible thing, as you understand."

"Yes," I said. "And then what happened?"

"Well," said Mrs. Crimmons, "he was some kind of ani-

mal, I guess. I don't understand at all, I really don't.
guess you people know about animals like this, but I . . .
well, I'm at a loss. It seemed forever that we were there,
and he gave me a cigarette and I was praying he would
let me go, but he didn't. He kept me there and after
we smoked, well, he attacked me again and then again.
It was like a nightmare. I couldn't believe it was happening."

"And then what happened?" Frank asked quickly in the
pause.

"Well, then he told me to go into the front seat again,
and then he drove around for a while and stopped in front
of this perfectly dreadful tavern, and he took me inside
and he ordered some drinks and . . ."

Frank and I looked at each other, and I asked the
question. "Were there other people in the tavern?"

Mrs. Crimmons studied a speck of light shining on the
arm of her golden chair. Her voice seemed to have
changed: not anger, but more than annoyance edging out
the soft, gentle quality. "There were people there, yes,
but not exactly the sort of people one would appeal to.
Several rough-looking men, a few dreadful women. You
know the type."

I kept my face very still, consciously controlling my
expression, for I know my features are very mobile, very
revealing. I avoided Frank's face with great effort, for I
knew he had turned toward me.

"And then," she continued, "we each had some drinks.
I don't know how many, it was all so unreal, and then we
went back to the car and he pushed me out after a while,
and I fell on the sidewalk. I don't know how long I
was there, and then that car—that officer's car—came and
stopped, and I was terrified until they told me they were
detectives. They took me to the police station and wanted
me to go to the hospital, but I told them that I just wanted
to go home—not see any doctor. It was just too terribly
humiliating. They were very pleasant, and one of the
nicest young officers took me home. I told him I felt that
I would be better able to discuss it today and, as you

see, I am rather calm about it now. But still, it was such a terrible thing."

Frank glanced at his notebook. "That was at 3 A.M. that the officers found you?"

"Yes, I suppose that's correct if that's what you have written in your book."

Frank ignored the reproach. "From twenty minutes to eleven till 3 A.M.—nearly four and a half hours."

Mrs. Crimmons moved slowly in her chair, digging her body in deeper. "I suppose so—it seemed like forever to me."

"Yes, and during all that time I imagine you had some conversation with him?"

Her eyes swung toward me, but her head still faced toward Frank. "Conversation? Well, of course, I pleaded with him, I begged him to let me go, if you consider that conversation."

"And what did he say? I mean, besides the threats. After the attack, what did he talk about?" My voice was flat and expressionless.

Mrs. Crimmons lit a cigarette and blew the smoke out quickly. She narrowed her eyes through the smoke. "What do you suppose he talked about?" she asked harshly. "What do people generally talk about in the back seat of a car parked in a dark alley?"

Frank's voice was polite and reasonable. "Did he say anything about himself? Anything that might give us some indication as to what he does, where he lives, his occupation?"

She blew the smoke from her lips in quick little puffs. "I will tell you this: times have changed." She waved the smoke from her face in agitated little pushes. "Young men do not behave the way they did when I was a young girl. They talk abruptly; everything is quick and to the point. When I was a girl," Mrs. Crimmons said, comparing her rape to her previous experiences, "when I was a girl, a man made love kindly, with patience and consideration. With a sense of slow and steady and wonderful achievement. The young men of today are animals: cruel and self-seeking and abrupt and selfish."

Frank coughed and fumbled for his handkerchief, and Mrs. Crimmons seemed not to notice; she was studying the puffs of smoke that formed all around her face.

The softness had gone completely from her voice. Her face, in the light from the lamp beside the chair, was bitter, and all the sweetness and smile had gone. She had had, during the telling of her story, the warm and breathy quality of a sleeping child, and yet there had been, to my mind, an indefinable aura of depravity about her. Perhaps it was her eyes, large and blurry, shining not with a light but with a wetness, blinking slowly and heavily with the weight of the moist layers of color smeared on the lids and the thick, sticky beads of mascara. The application of bright blotches of red on her high, thin cheeks was more pathetic than depraved, and her lipstick, a yellow-orange shade, was higher on one side of her mouth and gave her entire face a kind of unbalanced, lopsided appearance.

And it was in her voice. We had listened to the sound of it, moving with the slurred words which ran together in a steamy, flowing heaviness. The woman spoke in a continuing swell of emotion; yet it was a contrived outrage. The inflection, a sort of pseudo-Southern sadness, seemed to be in the wrong places and for the wrong reasons.

As she spoke, Mrs. Crimmons moved her hands, the long fingers climbing like spiders along the silken edge of her wrapper, making vain and feeble attempts to hold the garment against her body. I realized with a kind of disbelief—and at the same time without surprise—that the woman had nothing under the shimmering garment but her own round, full body.

Her hair was a flashing red, and the roots were a pinkish-orange suggestive of the insistent gray that was struggling from the scalp. It was a thick mass, worn shoulder-length with wispy, crinkled bangs partially covering the lined forehead—altogether inappropriate for a middle-aged woman. Her whole manner was of one who had once been a genuine lady trying to convince the world that she was a lady still, and at the same time trying to convey that she was, more importantly and regardless of time, a woman.

She filled the room with a strong and particular odor: an indefinable indication of sexuality. It was a combination of a certain mixture of heavy perfume and certain emanations of her own body that were not evidence of an unwashed state, not simply that. It was an unmistakable odor of some deep and driving physical desire, need, want, lust. It was still something more: something twisted, something degenerate and wrong and unhealthy and sickening.

Yet I listened without expression: calm, attentive, nodding, making the occasional listening sounds demanded. I looked at my partner's face to see if he, too, were aware of it—this thing that could not be spoken of, but was real and present in the room. Frank's face was set into an odd frown, perhaps his idea of sympathetic interest. But his eyes were shining and alive now, and there was a certain tenseness about his mouth as this thing crept about us, enveloping us in its weight.

Frank was aware of it, too.

I snapped open my pocketbook, removed another sheet of folded paper. "Can you give us a description of the man, Mrs. Crimmons? The officers told us you were too upset last night."

The woman shrugged, ignoring the fact that her wrapper had slid open a few inches, revealing the soft division between her breasts. "It was dark. Good heavens, I didn't look at him, I was trying to imagine myself away from him, from this terrible nightmare."

"Well, perhaps we could help you describe him," Frank said blandly, concealing any feelings. "Was he young— early twenties, say?"

"Yes, I would say so."

"Dark hair?"

"Yes, dark," she answered, her eyes on Frank's black head, the warm intonations returning.

"Dark eyes—brown?"

Mrs. Crimmons crushed out her cigarette in a huge

blue ceramic ash tray beside her on the table. "Dark hair, dark eyes, dark intentions."

I felt a shudder between my shoulders, a kind of rankling. The tone was almost, though not quite, coy. Mrs. Crimmons was studying Frank in long, open sweeps of her moist eyes. Her mouth was slightly open, relaxed.

"Tall, short, medium, what?"

"Not at all tall, officer—rather like you—medium, though not so well built."

Frank brushed a beady stream of sweat from his cheek. It was warm in the room.

"Was he clean-shaven? Neat? Shabby?"

Mrs. Crimmons, facing me again, shrugged impatiently. The sound of her voice returned to hardness. "Of course he was clean-shaven. I would have been scratched to pieces otherwise." She ran a hand down each cheek. "The way he kissed me, you see."

I nodded. "How did he speak?" Frank asked. "Any accent? Well-spoken? What was his voice like?"

"He had a thick way of talking, you understand—grunting, harsh, uneducated. Not like your voice. I would characterize your voice as, well, gentle—masculine and deep, but gentle." She smiled, blinked, wet her lips quickly with the tip of her tongue. "I say this so you will have some basis of comparison, you see."

"Yes," Frank answered without looking up. I wondered what he was writing, and saw a dark frown and a slow flushing start up the side of his face and around his ears.

"Mrs. Crimmons, have you ever seen this man before, around the neighborhood, I mean?"

"No, of course not. What do you mean by that?"

"Nothing," I explained, "except that he seemed to know the neighborhood. You said he knew exactly where to go, and I thought you might have seen him, you know, hanging around the neighborhood."

"I do not make a habit of noticing loungers." Mrs. Crimmons' voice was cold and sharp, and her enunciation became false. "If you noticed this neighborhood . . . Policewoman Uhnak, isn't it? . . . you would be aware that this is not the kind of place where hoodlums of this sort 'lounge' or 'hang around.'" She repeated the expression with disdain.

"Yes. Well, what else can you tell us about him?" I asked, ignoring her frowning disapproval. "Anything at all you can recall that might help us in locating him? Did he have any scars, any outstanding thing about him that might help us?"

Mrs. Crimmons lit another cigarette and pulled her mouth downward as she dragged the smoke to the back of her throat. "He was a very vague, nondescript kind of person, the type you wouldn't be able to pick out in a crowd," she said, with something like defiance.

I noticed that Frank had stopped asking questions; he was fidgety, pulling at his collar and smearing round and square designs on the border of his notebook page. "You mean you wouldn't be able to recognize him?"

Mrs. Crimmons shrugged indifferently. "I doubt it."

My face gave me away; my voice was devoid of incredulity. "You mean you wouldn't be able to pick him out of a line-up? But you were with him for over four hours, in a bar with him . . ."

Mrs. Crimmons' face became hard, and her eyes glittered brightly. "I do not think I care for your choice of words, policewoman," she said elegantly. "I wasn't 'with him' as you put it. I was held captive by him."

Frank came to life; he had been listening. "Yes, of course, that's what Policewoman Uhnak meant. Surely, Mrs. Crimmons, you'd be able to pick him out of a group of four or five men." Frank's voice sounded dry, as if he were having trouble swallowing.

Mrs. Crimmons smiled sadly. It was amazing to watch her switch her voice and expression back and forth between Frank and me. "As I say, he was one of these nondescript persons: dark hair, dark suit, nothing attractive about him. I could describe a man I passed on the street, a man on the bus whom I had seen for a moment or two— if he were attractive. If he was of a certain type, if you follow me." Frank coughed; apparently he had tried to swallow and had hit that dry spot. "Like the late Mr. Crimmons—he was a *man,* you understand." There was a quality of pride and fondness now. "Large and virile and attractive with that 'something special' radiating from him like a glow." Mrs. Crimmons' eyes ran over Frank's sturdy compact body and then looked directly into his face. "I could describe you quite accurately, detective, right down to your toes." Then she paused a moment and brushed the air. "But not that little animal of last night—an absolute nonentity. I couldn't even do a passing sketch of him."

Frank's eyes stayed on hers for a moment, held; then his feet moved on the carpet, and he watched his pencil make meaningless strokes over a star he had drawn.

"Listen, let me get you two something, it seems dreadful sitting here all this time." Mrs. Crimmons rose quickly and brushed off my questions about the car: some nondescript four-door thing. Black, maybe; some cheap make; who knew? Walking across the room, conscious of Frank's eyes on her body as the wrapper moved against her legs, she turned, coquettishly wagging a finger at him. "You're a Scotch man, detective. I always know a Scotch man."

Frank lifted his hand to protest, but she waved a finger at him graciously. "Never mind now, I insist." And then, belatedly remembering me, she softened with some effort. "And you, my dear, would you like something to drink? Good heavens, you seem so young to be a policewoman—to be involved in all this sordidness. I find it hard to understand how such a young girl could . . . Well, what would you like?"

Mrs. Crimmons was all warmth and charm and movement and soft sounds.

"No, thank you, Mrs. Crimmons, nothing for me."

The room was deadly still—she had carried it all out with her. In the emptiness, Frank rubbed his hand over his face, then rolled his eyes at me. I suppressed a grin, for he wasn't smiling. She came fluttering back into the room and held up a shot glass of amber liquid to Frank, and stood next to him as he tossed the Scotch down his throat. Then she handed him a glass of water, her eyes on his throat. Her own Scotch she sipped over some ice from a water tumbler, and it seemed to have no effect on her. Frank handed her the empty water glass and then finally mumbled, "Well, I guess that's all you can tell us, Mrs. Crimmons. We'll do what we can and keep in touch with you."

Mrs. Crimmons was smiling sadly. Her Southern sounds returned as she shook hands with me. "Yes, indeed, it was a dreadful thing, and I do appreciate you people coming out here. It's such a nuisance, I realize. I do wish I could help you some more, but there's really so little else to tell." She had reverted completely to the image she had initially presented. It was an amazing performance.

I pulled my hand from her wet clasp, but she didn't seem to notice. She was reaching for Frank's hand, her eyes, almost on a level with his, fastened on his lips, and his lips, feeling the impact of that wet stare, twitched slightly.

"Thank you so much. Detective Warener, isn't it? You've been so kind, and it's so very reassuring to know we have such fine police officers. I'm sure you'll do everything that you can. And let me know if I can be of any help to you. Anything at all that I can do for you, you let me know." And finally releasing his hand, she smiled and said softly, "I certainly would be able to describe you, detective."

Frank made a kind of gagging sound, pretending not to notice that one leg was exposed from the thigh to the ankle and that that leg was pressing against his own. He nodded and opened the door for me.

I stopped for a moment, a silly, childish feeling of nastiness prodding me. "Say, Mrs. Crimmons, I do a little sketching myself. I'd be very interested in seeing some of your work. Do you have any around?"

The shrewd eyes read my face; she ground her teeth together and spoke in a hissing voice. "I leave my sketch pad at Mr. Domingo's," she said.

"Oh, what a shame—I would have liked to have seen your work." I hesitated, then added meanly, "I'm sure you're a real professional."

The face folded into a network of hard wrinkles, and Frank's hand propelled me through the door, which slammed behind us. We heard the sharp jamming of a brass chain as the woman locked the door.

We walked down the patio steps and turned toward the corner where the car was parked. We walked nearly a full block before Frank stopped in the middle of the sidewalk and started to say something, then caught himself and shook his head, as though trying to wake himself up. "Jesus," he said, wonder and amazement and finally humor breaking into his expression. "Jesus! You know something, Dorothy, that's the first time my squad commander ever sent me on an assignment where I needed a policewoman as a bodyguard!" And he looked over his shoulder, back to where he had come through his ordeal safely.

We were laughing in gulps during the ride back to the precinct, latching on to words, insinuations, feelings, not even sharing them, and when we typed up our report, which was brief, terse and official, we ended it with one word: "Unfounded."

7

"Your only friend in all the world"

Like any other job, police work falls into set patterns: patrol this sector, cover this assignment, check this complaint, interview this man, this woman, this child, investigate this company, work on this case. But you are always conscious that the unexpected, the sudden violent event, is also part of the routine. If there is an undue hardness in the voice of the traffic cop stopping an offender for a minor violation, it might be because he remembers, in some deep part of his brain, hearing or reading of some cop, somewhere—stopping a light-jumper, a speeder, an improper turner—a cop who, summons book in hand, was shot dead. For no reason. If there is a dictatorial tone in the command of a policeman who tells a group of curious onlookers at some unusual event to move on, it might be because he has seen a curious crowd grow into a menacing mob. He has been part of it, has seen its ugly nature. In each arrest you make, you learn to take the initiative. It is essential. You take control immediately, and if your prisoner seems to be a nice guy, mild, calm, you don't give him any credit for his seeming meekness until he is safely deposited at the precinct. You learn not to relent, and you are aware that many police officers have failed in this lesson and lost their lives during a seemingly innocuous event that should have been merely "routine."

When I was given the assignment to work with Hank Ludlow, I was enthusiastic because it was an opportunity to work a regular day. A very regular day: 9 A.M. to 5 P.M.

The Kensington Shoe Company occupied a suite of

rooms in a modernistic glass building just off Fifth Avenue in the Fifties. The girls who worked there, the secretaries and shoe designers and models and assistants-to-vice presidents, were the type of women I had always avoided when possible. They were the grown-up little girls of my childhood, the clubby sophisticates of my adolescence: always sure, always right, chic, everything perfect. The right dress worn over the right sleek little garments; the sheerest stockings, always with a dull finish and never with a run; the played-down magical make-up that seemed to grow on their skin; the luminous eyes just indicating shadows; lipstick that never smeared, in shades that were beyond definite classification; and hair that fitted their heads, carefully casual, discreetly tinted with glistenings of color that subtly suggested sunshine. My feet ached in the unaccustomed high heels. When you patrol, you take refuge in flat, comfortable shoes. You wear warm bulky sweaters against the bitterness of nights, and hats that keep your ears covered.

I felt dressed up and ready for the theater, but this was how these girls dressed every day. I had spent extra time in the morning being careful with my make-up, and had walked around in my stocking feet until the last minute. I was supposed to be "one of the girls," and even knowing, realizing that it was just for the assignment, not for real, there was still that peculiar feeling of resentment, that old throwback rebellion of my tomboy days—not me!

We had interviewed the president of the company, Mac Gluttman—"Mr. Mac"—on Tuesday of the week. He was a short, stocky man with a square, blunt head lined on each side with cropped white hair. He had deep creases from his nose to his mouth, which turned heavily downward, and his elegant, custom-made suit fitted his Brooklyn-made body to perfection, emphasizing the thick shoulders and barrel chest.

"No crummy two-bit thief is gonna take me," he said, jamming his powerful thumb into his chest. When he spoke, an old-time venom took possession of his voice, and he seemed like some intruder—some roughneck—behind his shining, expensive long desk. "I know this type, I know this kind of bum, ya know." He leaned forward, shaking his head to advise us he was going to level with us—we would understand that he was no dumbhead. We were speaking to a self-made man who didn't get things handed to him on a platter; he was not to the shoe-business born. The hard way, that's how he got where he was. And where he was was at the head of a million-dollar fashion shoe outfit, the head of one of the sharpest, sleekest, shrewdest firms in the country.

"See those people out there?" He jutted that square jaw, prickly with tough white hairs, toward the paneled doors of his office. "Young. That's what I like around me. Young. Those girls—not one over twenty-five, including my two top designers. Young, that's what this firm is, and their president," thumping his chest, "is young, too. Sixty-four years old last May, and younger than the youngest one out there. I would take that bum myself, but my son," he turned and looked sourly at his replica, who stood motionless at his father's side, "he wants to do it this way. So you catch the bum, and don't let me get my hands on him—that's all I gotta say! Leo, you take them inside, in your office, and you tell them the score."

Mr. Mac slid his lower lip out as he studied me, ankles to knees, knees to waist, waist to neck, blinked quickly, dismissing my face, then down the line again. Then he nodded. I had apparently passed his strict inspection. "Yeah," he muttered. "Young—it's the best way to be, goddamn it. Ask me, I know."

"Mr. Leo" led us into his office, which was carpeted and quietly decorated by the same hand as his father's but was not nearly so lavish: he had not yet earned it. Mr. Leo was a weary man with lank black hair and his father's bullish shortness and shoulders and long arms which made him appear almost apish. He had smeary black rings under his eyes that extended down his cheeks and black, thick eyebrows that met over his nose and heavy, coarse lips. His fingers were yellow-stained and dirty, and the cuffs of his shirt were rimmed at their expensive edges with just a trace of grime. His manner was anything but young: he seemed too weary to last the day out.

"This guy, this window cleaner," he said, "three times now it's happened. I told the girls not to be so careless with their pocketbooks, with the petty cash. They think this is home; you know, it's not like an office—the carpeting, the couches, the upholstered chairs." Mr. Leo seemed to be expressing disapproval, and he was hunching forward, talking very quietly and glancing around from time to time. "They get comfortable, they relax, they forget, so they leave things around. My secretary, she lost her watch; my father's assistant, her wallet with sixty-seven dollars. A cigarette lighter, a junk jewelry ring, you know. And every time, that window cleaner was in here."

Hank Ludlow couldn't seem to settle his long frame on the foam rubber lounge. "How come you didn't call us before?"

Mr. Leo shrugged heavily, hunching his shoulders around his ears. "The old man . . ." He looked toward his father's office. "My father, he thinks he's Sherlock Holmes. He was gonna catch the guy. He'd throw him outta the window." Mr. Leo scowled like a stocky monkey. "Big deal—we're on the second floor. He's been playing detective, but nothing happens when he's around. The guy only takes something when the girls are in there alone—or the place is empty. Nobody seen . . . saw him take." He looked over his shoulder again. "He's been playing games, the old man. He's got a thing about being young, ya know?"

Mr. Leo held up his hand in a gesture that indicated we had some mutual understanding of what the "old man" was like. Leo had the beaten-down look of the son of his father.

Mr. Leo showed me to my desk. It was a huge, glass-topped, free-form thing, and I could see my feet sitting there on the floor, exposed to view, trying to settle themselves neatly. Everyone in the place seemed to have a big thing for feet, or rather for shoes. The girls all watched each other's shoes with hard, critical, professional eyes. Apparently, it was a rule that you didn't wear the same pair twice in a row. They knew immediately where I had bought mine and what I had paid for them, and I knew I didn't rate too highly with them on that account alone. There was a bright pink typewriter on my desk, looking like a toy. It was electric, and the keys danced wildly when I set my fingers on them.

The window-washer with the light fingers was due in the office sometime that day. He was finishing up the third floor and he always worked Kensington—it was his section. They didn't know exactly when he'd arrive, but I was hoping it would be soon.

Hank had asked why the girls hadn't complained to the man's boss, confront him with the accusation, even press charges, but the old man had insisted that he be caught in the act. Mr. Mac liked action, liked things done right, so there I sat at that crazy little pink typewriter and fooled around with the magic keys. Hank was in an adjoining office—the offices outside the executive suites were linked by airy, lacy white room dividers.

I did a few finger exercises to get the feel of the machine. I could see Hank looking over the sample shoes displayed on the wall-to-ceiling display case, fingering the fragile, needle-heeled high-style things with his large, unaccustomed hands. He held a shoe up to me, grinning; somebody's secretary, floating past, caught our amusement and froze in my direction, glancing quickly down. I tried to hide my feet but there they were on display under the glass desk. Then she raised her eyes to my face and looked right through me.

They spoke to each other in voices that were carpeted: soft, thick and expensively trained at one of those how-to-succeed schools which I had learned Mr. Mac insisted upon. He wanted them not only young but of a particular pattern. The only loud voice in the company was Mr. Mac's, and when he blasted forth on the small pink intercoms placed here and there on shelves about the room, everyone stood stock still, breathless, until he finished speaking. It seemed he had a technique all his own. Only when he finished the message would he announce the name of the person for whom it was intended. After an hour of these sudden pronouncements, I found myself listening intently, along with the others, as though it might be meant for me. "Those g.d. drawings are all smudges and smears and crappy, and I want the whole g.d. mess drawn up again. And play down the red edges. Marion!" "I want that showroom in one hundred per cent perfect order and no speck of dust showing and those new slippers —the pink ones and the off-green ones in K-13 case— right now. Harold!" It was a little upsetting.

There was no conversation with these girls. I was some-one who was just not there. They continued their quiet little gossipy huddles of office talk over drawings of shoes, pictures of shoes clipped from the best magazines—the kind that have a woman's face all over the page, sinking mysteriously into some kind of foggy background, and one word printed neatly in a corner, the name of a firm manufacturing some cosmetic or miraculous rejuvenation lotion. They might have stepped from some similar fog, and with their veiled, mean little glances, have wondered where I had stepped from. They knew I was a police-woman and drew certain inferences from this—probably that I was depraved and jaded from contact with the unspeakables of some remote and barely existent world.

I was wearing a little black dress, my "nothing" dress, with one small gold pin—a little owl Tony had found in the sand at Montauk—that was all grubby and chipped but had "Tiffany—14 k" engraved near the safety catch. He had had it cleaned and polished for me, and that little pin gave me a certain courage even if their rigid poise and rightness were somewhat unnerving. They all had noticed my feet with my unacceptable shoes, just plain black pumps and not expensive, but none of them had even looked at my good little gold owl. The hell with them. I would have lasted about a day in that place. I could feel the delicate wallpaper and antique picture frames—placed around little shelves of silly looking shoes —and the air of arduous refinement strangling me.

The window-washer came in from the reception room, wordless, and went directly to his task. As had been pre-arranged, the girls vaporized soundlessly without any sign of emotion, like a bunch of cardboard dolls floating effort-lessly away. Mr. Mac thundered from the walls for his secretary, and she glided over the carpet staring straight ahead, her notebook against her narrow, bony thigh. Hank was handling the shoes again, but he was watching me now, and I knew that he would keep his eyes on me until he received a signal.

I was typing some paragraph from some shoe news-paper, fascinated by the weirdness of the machine. It was typing with some strange power of its own, barely relying on my fingers. My back was to the window, but there was a lovely, wide-framed mirror perched on one of the room dividers that gave me a perfect view of the sus-pect. I could glance up from my machine easily and ob-serve him. He was smearing a squeegee over the pane of window from outside the building. He hadn't strapped on his safety belt, and he seemed to hang by the tip of one finger. I could hear him making grunting noises as he hefted himself inside the window frame and sloshed his arm up and down. I kept my fingers on the keys and they clicked furiously, in a frenzy of noise and activity. He had his back to me, bending over his bucket and rags and equipment, straps and buckles hanging from all sides of him. He ran a dirty gray rag over the back of his neck, then stuffed it into a back pocket. He leaned heavily on the desk alongside of him, rested his hand on the surface of the desk, and without looking behind him, toward me, pocketed the diamond engagement ring that had been left next to the pink telephone.

As I touched my hair, my left hand on the clicking keys of the machine, Hank started for the room. The window-washer reached into his shirt pocket, pulled out a cigarette and was placing it between his lips when Hank walked in and caught my nod and motion toward an imaginary pocket on my dress. I don't think Hank realized he was carrying the purple shoe in his left hand. He seemed a little surprised and let it drop to the floor as he took the window-washer's arm and stuck his shield in the man's face.

Hank was a tall man, deceptively swift while appearing

almost motionless. He had the suspect against a wall, or the latticework that passed for a wall, before I could even stand up.

"Put the bucket down, pal. Police."

Hank had one hand on the man's shoulder, and he jerked his head at the prisoner. "Okay, buddy, take the ring out of your pocket."

The man stared motionless but there was a whiteness coming over his face. Hank pushed the man's chest. "Take out the cigarettes and the ring. C'mon, c'mon, put everything on the desk."

"I got no ring," the man said tensely, his eyes wandering around the room, then back to Hank's face. He bit his lip, seemed to be weighing things, making some decision. "Not me, pal, I'm not your man."

Hank reached roughly into the pocket, tossed the cigarettes on the desk, then fished the ring out and held it before the man's eyes. "This yours?" he asked softly.

Hank motioned to me; the suspect seemed surprised to see me. He hadn't even noticed me. "I'm a policewoman. I saw you take the ring from the desk and put it in your pocket."

The voice of Mr. Mac suddenly boiled into the room, seeming to come from the ceilings and the floors. He had apparently been tuned in on us, and he was howling furiously about what he was going to do to the "bum." In the instant it took us to realize what the sudden sound was, the prisoner shoved Hank into me and lunged across the room. He crashed into the room divider and through the glass doors of the reception room into the hallway. I raced after Hank, grabbing my pocketbook from the desk, and saw Hank catch the glass door on his shoulder, fighting it back open. I heard the commotion on the stairway, a sound of ugly scuffling. Hank was hanging onto the straps that were dangling from the window-washer's pants, and the man kicked up with his heavy booted feet at Hank's legs. The stairway was hard steel, fireproof, and dangerous with sharp, point-edged steps. Hank had the man by the collar and I managed to grab a loose strap, but he shook me off with an elbow. I hadn't realized what a hugely powerful man he was, with arms and shoulders and back hardened by years of labor. He was a heavy-set man with no scrap of fat on him, and he made thick, grunting sounds. Hank was tall and wiry, but in the scuffling he lost his footing and tumbled on the stairs. The three of us fell together, Hank on the bottom, the prisoner on top. I fell clear of the men, pulled along by the strap which had gotten tangled around my wrist. I was clutching my pocketbook as though it were part of me, and I felt no pain even though I was aware of being pulled down the stairs. We all stood up together, still clinging to each other in one way or another, and fell against the brass door that opened onto the lobby of the building.

We exploded into the lobby into the midst of startled office workers on their way to lunch: three grappling, grasping figures. I had lost my shoes somewhere. I felt the cut on my leg, I heard the terrible sounds of blows—he was actually hitting *me*. My face felt the impact of the blow, but I felt no pain, just an awareness of having been struck. There was a terrible tangle of arms and legs; my hair was being pulled and I felt a hand inside my mouth, roughly scraping the roof of it.

"The gun," Hank gasped, unable to reach his own. "For Christ's sake, Dot, pull the gun."

I let loose my hold on the strap and dug the gun out, dropped my pocketbook somewhere. Hank managed to shove the man against the wall with his shoulder, holding him, leaning against him, trying to hold himself up, and I pointed the gun in the man's face. But I could see that the glazed, pale eyes did not recognize the weapon. It made no impression on him and his blank transparent expression was genuine.

"Sit still, you sonuvabitch, or I'll shoot you!"

He managed a kick at Hank's shinbone. I held the gun flatly in my palm, the finger off the trigger, as I felt myself being shoved halfway across the lobby. I landed against a candystand, and some face stuck itself in mine, some frantic candy-clerk face, saying words to me, hysterical words: "Lady, please, lady, get off my merchandise.

Lady, you're messing up my papers and my magazines."
I heard the words and the voice and saw the sickening
face, the arms outstretched over the shelves of candy
bars and gum, the voice wailing in grief for his magazines and newspapers and nickel and dime merchandise.
I saw all the faces all around us, a horrified, fascinated
group of faces, openmouthed, wide-eyed, drawing back,
yet too intrigued to move away—watching.

"Call the police!" I said in a thin, faraway, unknown
voice. "We're police officers; for God's sake, someone
make a call!"

Hank and the prisoner were grappling, and the powerful
man, using the advantage of his weight and conditioned
strength and those murderous dusty boots, delivered a terrific blow and kick at the same time. As Hank held on
to him, pulling him down too, I cracked the butt of my
gun at the base of his skull as hard as I could. It was
a horrible, loud, unimaginable sound, unreal. The window-
washer seemed to move in slow motion; he aimed a kick
at Hank, missed his footing, slipped to his knees, swung
his arm out wildly at Hank, who grabbed it and forced him
down. The back of his head, balding but with thin strands
of blond hair, began to ooze bright red from a long gash.
I kicked at his stomach, the sharp pain telling me I didn't
have any shoes on. He gave another animal lunge at me,
and I slipped backward, my feet skidding along the slippery polished floor. I felt myself making contact with
something, with someone, and some hands pushed me
angrily away. I turned. A woman, standing in back of
me, her face outraged, contorted, had pushed me. She
was pregnant, I could see that, it registered, but I couldn't
understand why she had pushed me. The prisoner and
Hank were on the floor, each making motions, reaching
for the other. As I moved toward them, some man, some
red-faced, tough-faced old man, some skinny wiry old guy
in a bank guard's uniform shoved his face at me.

"Cop?" That's all he said. I nodded, and he reached
down and gave the window-washer a terrific punch in the
face, and the prisoner settled down on the floor. Then the

man caught Hank's arms and pulled him to a sitting position and pushed his own face at Hank.

"Okay? Okay, officer?"

Hank nodded, not seeing the face before him, just nodding, maybe just trying to shake it off, to focus. He reached for his handcuffs, but the old guy snatched them away.

"I'll do it, pal." Quickly, professionally, he slipped the handcuffs on the prisoner, who was reviving, twisting. He cuffed the man's hands behind his back, explaining as he did so, "Six years off the force and I haven't lost the old speed. Heard the commotion. I'm at First National—right in the building. You okay, girlie? 70th Precinct in Brooklyn last ten years on the job. Hey, you okay, girlie?"

I nodded, not looking at him but at the crowd, at the faces that were watching us, watching us, talking about us, pointing at us, at Hank and the prisoner and the bank guard and me. I saw the uniformed cops come in through the revolving doors—four of them, then three more, then a sergeant, a big, fat sergeant with great big cheeks.

The uniformed cops grabbed everyone; the sergeant had my arm. I was still holding my gun. "Policewoman—sergeant—that's my partner, and this man here, he helped us."

The spectators moved a little closer, wanting to hear some more of it. They knew nothing of what was happening. Some woman, some woman from the crowd, whom I had never seen, kept calling to the sergeant, telling him she wanted to talk to someone in charge. She saw his stripes and kept on calling and calling until finally, with a heave of annoyance, he turned to her.

"Lady, what is it? Whassa matter—what d'ya want? C'mon, you men, get these people outta here—show's over—go to lunch." The woman, eyes blazing, pointed at us.

"I was a witness," she said in a high, shrill voice, and everyone came closer for a better look. "I want to know who to talk to here."

"Lady," the sergeant said, in his old-timer's growl, "what d'ya want?"

"I want to report an incident of police brutality," she said indignantly and shaking with rage. "I saw the whole thing: this girl hit that man on the head with a blackjack or a gun or something, and he was on his knees, helpless. Then this man, this bank guard, came and beat him mercilessly, and all the time his hands were handcuffed behind his back."

I started to speak, to shout. I knew the words were terrible, shocking, all the dirty words the kids at the settlement house had tried out on me, all the words the men tried to cut out of their daily conversations if I was assigned to work in a squad room. They felt good and satisfying and appropriate and expressive. They were a release and a pleasure, and I didn't care who heard me. I advanced on the woman, but the sergeant held my arm firmly and gave quick orders to the men. The uniformed officers mingled into the crowd and cleared everyone out.

The prisoner started to fight again, hands behind his back. He kicked out wildly, throwing his body against the blue uniforms, oblivious to the pain of the blows he received, unaware of them. Five officers pitted themselves against him, but he had some maniac strength, some desperate wild power, and they clobbered him repeatedly before they could drag him out of the building and into the paddy wagon.

"C'mon, holy terror," the sergeant said, "let's get up to that office and clean you two up. You got your coats up there?" And then he looked at my feet. "And your shoes?"

He had me by one hand and Hank by the arm with his other hand. Hank was dazed and wincing with pain. "Hey," he mumbled, "where's that little guy, that bank guard? He's a former cop."

But he had vanished, gone back to his own work.

There was complete silence when we entered the hallowed premises of the Kensington Shoe Company. I thought it was because I was carrying my shoes, which I had retrieved from the stairway. Then I realized they were looking at Hank and that his face was covered with blood. A uniformed man ran into the office, holding my pocketbook out to me. I checked that nothing was missing: shield, wallet, keys, make-up kit, address book. I dug for a comb. They just looked at me, those immaculate girls, speaking wordlessly to each other but saying nothing to me.

I went to the mirror to fix my hair and stared at myself. My face was filthy and my mouth was bloody. That was the salty taste, blood from a cut inside my mouth. It was all over my chin and the back of my hand and had gotten smeared into my hair. There was a tenderness on my cheek, and I could see a soft blue swelling. Damn them, watching me, damn them. I whirled around, primed, furious, and they dropped their eyes and the sergeant had my arm again.

He grinned at me fondly. "Hey, you're a little terror, all right. Go into the ladies room and wash your face. And for God's sake," he said sternly, "put on your shoes. Seems we're in some kind of holy sanctuary here, and there you stand in your runny stockings!" He said it loudly in his booming street voice, and I loved that sergeant for bringing forth those shocked expressions at his boisterous irreverence.

"I hate shoes," I said. "I think they're for the birds!"

It was my judgment of them, and I was finished brooding about their weighing of me. To hell with them, all of them. I walked stiffly out of the room, staring them down. After I had washed up in the ladies room, I came back to the office, still carrying my shoes. Somehow, I could not put them back on—not yet.

The sergeant was arguing loudly with Mr. Mac, shouting him down. "I don't give a damn if you can't spare her, she's the complainant and she's gonna sign the complaint."

An icicle of a girl in a navy blue knit dress with white pearls studied the sergeant's florid face with interest. To her, it was a strange, upsetting visage. Mr. Mac waved his arm at the sergeant, who caught it mid-air. "Don't wave your hands at me, mister. Miss, is this the ring the guy took? Is it yours? Did you leave it on that desk?"

The girl nodded silently, once to each question, then

waited for Mr. Mac to give further answer. "But you got him, and that's it as far as we're concerned. No court for my girl, and that's it, that's it. Final. Finished. She's needed here and that's that. My attorney will get the ring back at the precinct, so don't threaten to withhold it on me."

And no matter what the sergeant said, or how he said it, we were to have no complainant. It was our case, and they were out of it. I put on my shoes finally and got my coat and noticed that Hank, sitting wordless on the couch, was drawn with pain and that he was rising carefully and stiffly. I was beginning to hurt, too: my legs and my face and my mouth and my hands. We made less than a triumphant exit, but I turned and glared at them at the door, knowing they would all be looking at us. I put as much contempt and scorn and distaste as I could summon into my look, but I could feel my mouth swelling and I must have looked pretty grotesque. My hand went to touch my owl: he was gone. Somewhere in the scuffle, my little gold owl had gotten lost and I felt a deep, panicky sense of loss. He would never be found.

The sergeant had a patrol car waiting at the curb and directed that we be driven to the nearest hospital; the prisoner was at the precinct waiting to be booked. A crisp, dark-skinned Indian intern told me to take off my stockings: they were ripped to shreds and my legs were scraped and dirty. I hadn't noticed the cut across my right ankle. He cleaned me off with some clear lotion spilled on pieces of sterile cotton, and my eyes filled with tears at the sting. Then he stained me with some red medication. They took Hank off in another direction, and I had noticed he was bending over, leaning toward his right side.

The intern had a clear, smooth face—alert, unsurprised, thoroughly professional. "You are a policelady, yes? Very interesting. Do you hurt anywhere else? Any parts of your body? Did you fall, land on your back? H'mm, very interesting." His accents were carefully British and polite, but distant and cold.

He gave me some bitter medicinal lotion to swash

around in my mouth and spit into the small round steel sink.

"Have you ever had a TAT?" Then he explained evenly, "Tetanus anti-tetanus injection?"

"No."

"Well, I will give you three injections, you understand? A divided dosage. We will then wait thirty minutes between injections; if you have an allergy to this, there will be a red swelling the size of a . . . ah . . . quarter, yes, and we will not give you any more. So." He jabbed the first dose into my right arm, on the inside just below the elbow. Then he disappeared, making soft little sounds with his mouth. A nurse came and took down the facts they needed for their records and gave me a paper to sign—a release of some kind. I asked about Hank: she didn't know. I stretched out on the hard examining table. The intern came back exactly thirty minutes later, looked at my arm and gave me a second injection. An older doctor came, a funny-looking man with long gray hair and a clean white coat. He looked at my arm, at my bruised legs, smiled at me vacantly, murmured, then became busy at a desk. I asked him about my partner.

"He's having some X-rays; has some pain in his back and shoulder. He's in good hands." He smiled contentedly, a wide, yellow-toothed look.

The nurse came back and smiled at me. "Well, you'd better pretty up. There are some reporters out there, and they want to take your picture," she chirped.

Two men came in, one carrying a camera, and they were directing the doctor to pose with me. The one with the notebook was asking me how to spell my name, how old I was, my partner's name, the prisoner's name. I realized, with some shock, that I didn't even know the prisoner's name, but the reporter said they'd check at the precinct. He asked a few quick questions and then was satisfied with my answers. Then the photographer began placing us for the picture. The old doctor got a grip under my chin and pushed my head back so that all I could see was the ceiling. The photographer kept hiking up my skirt and I kept pulling it down. Straining my eyes, I could see the toothy yellow grin of the doctor. The photographer told him to lower my face a little—all he could see was my neck. And my knees. The doctor jerked my head an inch or two lower, but his grip was so strong I couldn't see the photographer, just the flashes of light which left circles of blue before my eyes. Then the reporters took off.

The old doctor disappeared with the reporters and I didn't see him again. I didn't want to call Tony at his office; I'd wait until I knew he was home. My arm started to feel a little peculiar. There was a round circle of bright red on my inner arm. It was very hot and tender and itchy, and the circle was raised almost a quarter of an inch. Great. The Indian intern wasn't in the hallway but he was due back in about ten minutes. On the dot, he arrived, his needle pointing at me. The red circle had disappeared by this time.

"Doctor, there was a bright red circle there a few minutes ago," I told him, pulling my arm from his hand.

He studied me with his liquid brown eyes. "Ah, very interesting. Now, when you say 'bright red,' ah, what exactly do you mean?"

I clenched my teeth. "Bright. Red."

"So. And how large was the, ah, circle, please?"

I made a circle with my thumb and index finger. "And it was very hot, very red and very hot."

He shrugged, a graceful gesture. "What you say is bright red, very hot, ah, might not be what I say is, ah, bright red and very hot, you see? Did the nurse examine it?"

I wanted to get out of there: to go home. "Nobody saw it. *I* saw it. It was *red* and *hot,* just like you said to watch for."

"Ah, but I must see this for myself," he said, calmly ignoring my testimony. "You cannot judge this thing," he said with maddening superiority. "I will give you the last portion of the TAT." And he did so before I could protest and then he left, having completed his job.

I could feel the fluid that had been forced into me against my will, and I was overwhelmed by a feeling of helplessness and self-pity. They had knocked me downstairs, pushed me from their lousy candystand, shoved me away, stared and pointed at me, accused me of brutality, dismissed my best dress and stolen my only really good gold pin. Their scornful eyes had looked right through me, and now they were pumping me full of some kind of poison!

I started to cry, a wet noiseless mixture of anger, frustration, hurt, pain and heavy body-aching weariness. I washed my face in the sink and looked at myself in the antiseptic steel-framed mirror. Only my eyes were familiar —still grayish-blue, but the whites were red veined. My nose was shiny, there was an irregular greenish-yellow lump on my cheek, my lower lip was swollen like a petulant child's, my hair was streaked with the dirt of the stairway and blood from my own wounds and the prisoner's. I was a mess, and to top everything off, they had taken my picture for the newspapers looking like some beaten contender.

You feel, sitting in an examining room of a busy hospital, with people coming in and out of the room, racing about the halls, pushing their important trays of medicines and needles and equipment, that you are completely alone, forgotten, without identity beyond the extent of your wounds. It is their world, the doctors and nurses and attendants and admittance clerks, and they don't answer your questions and they don't do anything beyond tending the immediate, physical evidence of your needs. Finally, I called Tony from a phone booth in the hall. He had just received a call from my sister who had heard a news report on the radio giving a brief run-down of the arrest, in which my name had been mispronounced, of course.

My words were careful and calm; my voice was flat and without emotion. I told him where I was and that I was all right, just a little tired. Yes, I was sure. We'd talk about it later. Oh, and I was a little bruised. It was okay, really it was, I was mostly very tired. I didn't know when I'd be home. It was after six, and I still had to book the prisoner and write up reports and God knows what else. I would keep in touch by phone.

They did some X-rays of my skull. I hadn't known they were going to, but found out when a bustling white starchy nurse pushed a wheelchair at me, ignored my indignation, planted me in it and propelled me down the hall and into an elevator. The wheelchair was pushed down another hall, then came to a halt alongside a mobile table. Hank was stretched out on his stomach, his head resting on his arms, his eyes closed. His long, weather-beaten face was gray, his mouth drawn down in pain.

"Hey, Hank," I called softly, not sure if he was sleeping. He opened his eyes dully. "You okay?"

"They gave me something," he said dreamily. "Something to ease it up. Boy, my back is still killing me. And damn it," he moaned, "my good suit. My jacket is ripped. Not the seam—a big hole right in the center of the back—isn't that a killer?" He shook his head dreamily and seemed to be trying to remember something. "Oh hey, Dot, listen, will you call my wife? You have my home number. Listen, just tell her I'm all right. Don't tell her about the X-rays, just say they're going to keep me overnight. The station will call her, but maybe if you just talk to her—you know." Then, blinking his eyes wide open, "Hey, Dot—how are you? You okay? What did they do for you?"

I told him I was fine, but that they had probably poisoned me with those divided injections. It was nice to be able to tell somebody.

"Hey," he said, his eyes closed, "you were swell. Really, kid, you were right in there."

It made me feel a little better. It was the kind of praise usually grudgingly given—they feel a girl is deadweight in a rough arrest.

"You know, Hank, in the tussle I think I might have kicked you once or twice—all those arms and legs."

He was silent a moment. Then he lifted his face, smiling, and chuckled. "Wow, you sure told them off, didn't you?"

I felt my face burn. I had forgotten, and the angry words which I had shouted at the crowd flooded back. "Well, please don't quote me, Hank. I was pretty upset. I don't even remember exactly what I said. Besides, I didn't think you were in any condition to hear me."

"I heard you, all right, and believe me, you used all the right words. Perfect."

Then he seemed to doze; the medication was taking effect. I was wheeled into the X-ray room, and when they pushed me out, he was gone. Back downstairs, they released me and I called his wife. Her voice was small, quiet, frightened in my ear. She asked me over and over again, "But he's all right, isn't he?"

"He's more worried about his good suit than anything else, Mrs. Ludlow. You come by and see him tomorrow morning and bring a needle and thread, and then he'll be great."

Hank Ludlow spent two months in the hospital with two broken vertebrae and a dislocated shoulder. I was luckier: nothing broken.

When I reported back to the precinct, I learned our prisoner had gone berserk when they attempted to fingerprint him in the detectives' room. He had smashed ink bottles all over the place, turned over a heavy desk, smashed a chair before they got him handcuffed to a radiator and called for the psychos. By the time they arrived with a straitjacket, he had battered his knuckles against the radiator until they bled, then started on his head, splitting gashes across the forehead. The squad commander wouldn't let anyone near him: let him make his own bruises. It took four men quite a time to get him secured into the straitjacket, and he took to snapping his teeth at the interns when they tried to wrap up his bleeding head. A check of his record at the Bureau of Criminal Identification showed two previous arrests for felonious assault. I typed up my report and filled out my arrest cards, then called Tony to tell him that I was on my way. He wanted to come for me in the car, but I wanted to get going right away; he could meet me at the subway station. I kept my face down, hiding my bruises, watching the people—the subway riders, the citizens—staring blandly at each other, at their newspapers filled with violence and blood and crime, flipping the pages, wetting fingers for continuations of stories. A small colored boy danced through the train selling morning papers at twice the newsstand price. I bought a *Daily News,* and there was a picture of the doctor and me on page four and a brief run-down on the arrest. I looked at other people reading the story, taking it all in, *all of it* in one quick glance, knowing the whole story, and then passing on to something else.

I checked at the precinct the next morning and was surprised to learn that the prisoner was able to be arraigned. They had called the hospital prison ward, and I was to meet a detective within an hour and escort the prisoner for mug shots and to court.

He was silent when I saw him, his bandaged face pressed to his chest. His hands were encased in bandages and were handcuffed on his lap. He looked up when I entered the hospital room, blinked his swollen eyes in some confusion, then smiled.

"You're the lady cop, huh?" There was a peculiar admiration in his voice. I didn't answer him. "Boy, what a battler. Hey, who was that other guy—that one who bashed me in the face? That little old guy. Jeez, I didn't do nuthin' to him!"

And there we were, having a conversation just like normal, sane people do, and I even found myself asking him how he felt. He moaned. He was feeling the pain now, as I was. The full extent of all his batterings, from us, from himself, had descended on his body now, and he said he ached all over. Then he asked how I felt. I said okay.

"You the one split my head open? Whatd'ya hit me with?" He was curious, respectfully curious.

The detective made a slight sound—a warning. "With my hand, mister. I'm a karate expert." The prisoner whistled softly and didn't talk any more during all the processing.

At court, when the case was called, the detective got him from detention, and there was a stir in the courtroom when he appeared, looking like the movie invisible man, only the bandages giving him form. A slim, well-dressed man bobbed up from somewhere to represent him. He waved to Sessions, and the prisoner, quiet now, quiescent, was taken away.

I saw the attorney talking with a faded blonde woman who kept staring at me while listening to him in the corridor outside the courtroom. As I walked past them, the attorney caught my arm, smiling.

"Officer Uhank, isn't it?" he said pleasantly.

I corrected him and he apologized, then introduced me to the woman. "This is Mrs. Schmidt—Ralph's wife." We regarded each other warily. "Listen, Policewoman Uhnak, I want to talk to you a minute, get a run-down on this thing. You know how the newspapers louse things up, and I didn't get a chance to talk to Ralphie yet. Boy, you people sure clobbered the daylights out of him, didn't you?" he asked with a sly laugh.

I pulled back from him, feeling nasty and bruised and belligerent. "Talk to your client, counselor. I have nothing to say to you. You heard the affidavit."

He ran after me, leaving Mrs. Schmidt in the middle of the hallway. "Hey now, young lady, don't get me wrong. I know that old Ralphie is a little—well, rough. That poor woman puts up with a lot. But you know, he didn't used to be that way."

"I saw his record," I replied coldly.

The attorney brushed the record aside with a wave of his hand, and spoke in that infuriatingly confidential tone they use to dazzle their befuddled clients: only to *you* do I reveal these things; only *you* would understand. "They had a big tragedy, you see. Five years ago, they had this kid, and the boy wasn't right, you know." He touched his head. "You know, you know. Well, they spent a fortune on that kid—doctors, phonies, diets, tests, prayer-phonies, the whole thing—and the kid died when he was two years old. Ralphie went off the deep end, became a wild man. He hasn't been right since. Believe me, I know this guy—known him for years. He's a good, hard-working stiff and every now and then," he said matter-of-factly, "he goes off."

"Like copping things from desks and fighting the whole world?"

The attorney's bright eyes winked. "Now, officer, you haven't got a grand larceny and you know it. We'll cop out to petit—you haven't even got a complainant."

"I'm the complainant. I saw the larceny."

He smiled knowingly. "You won't make a grand larceny stick."

I knew he was right, and it made me all the more determined. "We'll see." I started to walk away again. He caught my arm.

"Now about the assault—you're not badly hurt. Hell, look at what you guys did to Ralph—the poor slob's a mess. Even the picture in the paper—you see him in the center of the late *News?*" I pulled away, and he called after me down the hall, "It'll be reduced to simple assault, officer. He's really a good guy."

And, of course, Schmidt's attorney was right. The larceny *was* reduced to petit larceny, and the felonious assault *was* reduced to assault in the third degree, and they copped out to a 30-day sentence in the workhouse. Any cop can tell you that an assault on a police officer counts for nothing. It is almost always reduced to third degree. Except if the suspect kills you, and then they give you a big funeral with a color guard and a flag and lots of uniformed men in attendance.

Two days later, I arrived home a few minutes after Tony. (They put me on light duty for a week.) All my pains were throbbing. Tony's face was pale with anger. "Did you see this?" he asked, shoving the evening paper at me, folded back to the letters-to-the-editor page.

There was a one and a half column letter signed by a Mrs. Anna Kempler and headed: DISGRACEFUL POLICE BRUTALITY! Mrs. Kempler had put down the angry words of the righteous citizen, calling attention to the disgraceful incident she had witnessed in the lobby of the building where she had worked, day after day, for fifteen years, and never, never had she seen anything so frightening, so disturbing, so outrageous. These two men and one girl, pounding and beating this helpless man who had not done anything, not a thing. She knew, she had seen the entire incident from start to finish. Somebody had better do something about this. Somebody had better find out about this. This was not the 1930s, after all. And the sergeant had tried to cover up the whole thing. She was sending a copy of this letter to the mayor and the police commissioner and to all the newspapers. That's how strongly she felt about this dreadful incident in our city.

I handed the paper back to Tony and he flung it into the wastebasket. I sat down in a chair, my legs over the arm, my head back, looking at the ceiling. I held my hand up when he started to speak.

"No, wait," I said, "I have a better one for you. Sergeant Cornelius—you know, that nice big loudmouth I told you about—he called me at the Bureau office today." I put my hand over my eyes, I was talking into my chest. "He was notified that the Corporation Counsel's office has received a notice of claim. A notice of claim." I shook my head.

"What does that mean?" Tony asked.

I stretched and yawned. "It means that that woman, the pregnant woman I got pushed into—I mean whom I 'assaulted,' it turns out she is the wife of an attorney with offices in that building. They put their scheming little heads together and decided that in case she has a miscarriage between now and the next two months, they intend to have the city pay them enough to build themselves a nice new house and give themselves a vacation in Bermuda or maybe a trip around the world—or maybe to the moon. I don't know."

Tony flung his lighter on the table and looked around for a match. "I don't get it, what do you mean?"

"Well, they filed a notice of claim, put the city on notice that this poor pregnant woman, standing there in a public place, waiting for her husband to take her to lunch, was caused 'grievous bodily harm' by this police officer, and that if she suffers a miscarriage the city, on behalf of this police officer, shall be required to pay her upward of a million bucks!"

"God damn!" That was all either of us could think of to say or were willing to put into words. We didn't bother with supper. Neither of us was hungry, and I was beginning to get a nagging pain in my right side: a nipping, biting little pain which was getting a little too persistent to ignore. I took the few phone calls from relatives and friends; explained, rather shortly, that I was fine. No, I hadn't heard it on the radio; yes, I did save the pictures and articles from the newspaper.

The next day I received a summons at the Women's Bureau to go home and get into uniform and present myself at headquarters for an interview with some inspector from the Commissioner's office. They were acting on a request from the mayor in response to Mrs. Kempler's special delivery, registered letter.

A stenographer took down my statement as the inspector interrogated me without expression—just the facts as I reported them. He advised me that a statement had been taken from Hank Ludlow at the hospital. He didn't tell me not to worry, just had me wait until the typist wrote up the report. I signed it and checked back to the Women's Bureau, finished my tour, and went home.

My bruises healed in time, although that TAT shot caused some trouble. Two weeks after it had been administered, I noticed a sense of heat in my right upper arm. I took off my sweater and was startled to see a huge red swelling, a kind of tight band hugging my arm. I was headachy, irritable, and within an hour, started to feel "out of things"—not with it. My speech became forced and stammering and unnatural. I called the hospital and reported to the nurse in charge. She advised me, in tones somewhat less than reassuring, to report to the hospital immediately. Tony took me to our family doctor, and he administered some drugs to fight off the poison in my system.

Apparently, the attorney's wife had her baby without unusual difficulties. At any rate, I never heard anything further about their notice of claim turning into a full-fledged suit.

Mrs. Kempler's accusations in the newspaper went unanswered. The police department was satisfied that we had acted properly and issued a report to the mayor's office, and carbon copies were inserted into Hank's and my personnel folders. That was to serve as our official vindication. Officially, we had taken proper police action.

During the week I stayed home on sick report, nursing the headaches and feelings of disorientation and heat, I had a lot of time to think—about people, and who they are and what they do, or do not do, and why. Tony and I had rehashed it to the point of frustration: it only led to empty anger, and at whom? Who wants to get involved? Who wants to take a chance? Who wants to know about things?

What could you do—write a letter to the editor? No. You pass it all by and chalk it up to experience.

8

"I have grown hard, and my heart has turned to stone"

Everyone thinks he has premonitions or foresight, based on thoughts or feelings he seems to remember having had before an event actually occurred. Thinking over some significant event, some large or unusual or disastrous or wondrous happening, our minds glide and waver backward and forward in time, and we believe we did have some mysterious hint, some forewarning. I'm not sure if these things are genuine or if they're just a mixed-up jumbling, a misplaced kind of remembrance. But I do know that I had this kind of feeling about my Fulton Street assignment. I *knew* from the first interview I had that I was to be the one to catch the man who had beaten, robbed and viciously attacked several women in the recesses of the intricate tunnelings of that far downtown subway station. I even believe that I mentioned this to Tony after that interview with the director of the Policewomen's Bureau, but he doesn't seem to recall the particular discussion.

I had, of course, seen the director many times in the office, walking briskly about her business, her slim body erect and businesslike. I had had some glancing pangs of envy, tempered, perhaps, by an awareness that her job was not an easy one. I was only slightly aware of the pressures placed upon her. She kept herself apart, and she was subject to criticism for her stiff insistence on formality. We were always Miss So-and-so or Mrs. So-and-so, and even her secretary was devoid of a first name. She interviewed three of us who had been selected, I suppose, on the basis of our records or immediate availability. During my interview, she sat behind her desk, neatly filled with stacks of paperwork and charts and sharpened pencils and shining ash trays (she did not smoke, nor did anyone who entered this domain), and spoke briefly and to the point, glancing once at her wrist watch and then increasing her speed.

"It is admittedly a dangerous assignment," she said, "and while it is not open to volunteers, I will give the girl selected an opportunity to decline without prejudice." I nodded, believing her, and she spoke without passion. "The culprit," she stated in official police language and referring to a report before her, "has attacked these women viciously, has rendered two of them unconscious: two rapes, one sodomy and three beatings. He is armed, once used a knife on a victim, and on all other occasions displayed a revolver. You would be assigned, of course, with a very competent detective from the 1st Precinct, and would have good coverage." She held up a maplike drawing to me. "If you are assigned—and accept the assignment—you will have to become familiar with the Fulton Street station. It is a hub station: the BMT, IRT and Independent Subways all cross here, accounting for the great number of tunnels and passageways. Apparently, according to the location of the various attacks, the mugger prowls about the station and attacks wherever he locates a victim." And then she regarded me levelly, her face noncommittal; "I will let you know tomorrow if you are to be assigned, and you will let me know your feelings." And I was dismissed by her quick glance at her wrist watch and her pushing aside of the subway map in favor of some papers requiring her signature.

And so, the following morning, it was given to me like a prize, and I accepted it like a prize, not concentrating on her words but glancing down at the map in my hands. "Mrs. Uhnak, I will caution you just once in this matter: it is not going to be easy. Your record shows you to be very competent, but I will warn you to take all necessary precautions. In other words"—my head shot up at her sudden cold tone—"no grandstanding. Good luck." She dismissed me abruptly and expected no answer, and I rode to the 1st Precinct brooding over her words. Then

I pushed them aside, feeling the excitement go through me like a tonic. I spoke to the squad commander of detectives, was introduced to my partner, and sent home after being told that this was a 4 to 12 assignment.

My partner was a man named Paul Durkee. He had a tremendous, fat face with pendulous red cheeks, and the sockets of his eyes were incredibly big. His blue eyeballs swam around loosely, as though looking for some safe harbor, but at no point did they touch the edges of the sockets. Speaking to him, or rather listening to him—for he was a compulsive talker—I found myself stretching my own eyes wide, subconsciously trying to match his. He told me endless stories, in a rapid succession of words and in unrelated bits and scraps with many whisperings and mutterings. He covered his mouth with his beefy hand, his eyes wandering wildly, so I was sure he was revealing the most confidential information imaginable in the realm of the police department's history—but I couldn't follow anything he told me. He gave an odd little click at the end of every gasp of information, and at the end of two tours with him, I found myself beginning to click, too. It is a terrible weakness of mine: picking up other people's mannerisms, gestures, intonations and habits. I feel myself doing it, time after time, echoing someone else's choice expletive, in *his* tone of voice, with *his* expressions and motions.

Working with Paul Durkee was quite an experience. While he was excessively heavy, even for his large frame, he was quick on his feet and in endless motion. We patrolled the station from end to end, up and down the intricate stairways, racing about as though pursued by demons. Durkee had an air of impending doom. Everyone was suspect and was thoroughly examined by his rolling eyes. He was full of secret signals, nodding, motioning, jerking his thumbs, pushing his hat back or forward, taking it off, smashing it back on. I couldn't figure out what he was doing, or what I was supposed to do in response, but apparently my just standing motionless and observing him fitted into his scheme of things, for he never spoke about my lack of reaction. Watching him hurrying down the platform, his great bulk a massive shadow on the dark platforms, he seemed like a living oval: very wide in the middle and tapering at each end. I had met his son in the squad room the first day we worked together: a pale, limp little boy with wet hands who slipped his hand into mine on a signal from his father, let it drip there for a moment, then removed it with a little nod of his curly head. His father, beaming and roaring above him, was very proud of his son's fine manners. He seemed to me for all the world like some little trained monkey, for the boy was completely devoid of expression and took his actions strictly from his father's wild signals. Paul thumped the boy on his thin back and winked one crazy eye and thundered: "That's my boy—Turkey Lurkey Durkee."

The relationship between partners, even in a temporary arrangement, is a delicate thing, particularly when you are together on a potentially dangerous assignment. Though Durkee strained my ears and nerves and credibility to piece together his stories, at the center of our working relationship was the definite knowledge that Paul Durkee was what you'd call a "stand-up" guy. He was there. He was a full, complete, entire cop, and no matter what happened or what you encountered, Durkee would be right there, in the middle of it. You get to know a lot about a man in eight steady hours—eating together, patrolling together, watching each other. I knew that Durkee was loud and boisterous and given to boasting about his past achievements, but I knew, aside from all that, that he would live up to his claims.

By the fourth night, we both started to get a little stale. There was no action, nothing was happening. You start out at top pitch, expectant and ready, but the hours grind you down. Durkee slowed down a little. Not his eyes, which kept racing wildly up and down the platforms, seeming able, almost, to penetrate the walls and see around corners. But he slumped on a bench occasionally, his thick legs stretched before him, his hat tilted over his face, his eyes, probably, peering through the felt. He could sense the approach of a subway train long before there were any faint rumbling vibrations, the vibrations that

grew into echoes and then into the full thunder of a train
entering the station. And his whole posture changed, almost without movement, into a waiting and a watching.
Then his body would relax, again without moving, and
we would observe the doors slide closed and the train
leave the station.

We went for a meal at eight o'clock; our relief was a
wiry old detective with a bad cold who complained bitterly that the steel dust was bad for his allergy. He proved
his point by sneezing wetly all over us and blowing his
nose like a trumpet.

"You have walking pneumonia," Durkee told him,
shaking his head. "Can kill you like that!" He snapped
his fingers at the relief man, shook his head again,
grabbed my arm suddenly and dragged me along with
him.

At the restaurant, a dimly lit greasy joint, Durkee, his
face flushed and puckish, started a loud conversation in
the middle of nowhere, widening his eyes. "You'd just
better not let me catch you with that bum again, that's all
I'm gonna say about it!" he bellowed.

And the waitress, a fat redhead jammed into a greenish
nylon uniform, looked quickly at me, then at Durkee, then
at me again, her eyes blinking. She raised the pencil in-
quiringly at me and Durkee pulled the menu out of my
hand and thrust it at her.

"I'll order for *her*," he said. "Give *her* a rare burger
and a cuppa tea. I'll have the specialty—beef stew and
some extra French fries on the side!"

He waved the waitress away with his heavy hand, and
she glanced back at us, her face puzzled. Durkee winked
at me.

"See? She thinks we're just a typical married couple."

It was his way of stirring things up, for we were both
weary and stiff from the endless hours of patrol. He en-
joyed playing little games, creating impressions and play-
acting. I ate the hamburger—which was what I always
ordered—without tasting it. There was an odd feeling of
tension, starting somewhere on my right side and traveling
into my chest and hitting the back of my throat. An oddly

familiar warning sign: something going to happen; something not right.

I called Tony before we returned to our post, and he caught my mood, my vague, uneasy sense of caution. "You okay, Hon?" he asked. Of course. I am always okay. And then, just before I hung up, he said, "Listen, you take care of yourself; you stay close to that nice big partner of yours, okay?"

Durkee bought himself an early edition of the morning paper; it was eight-thirty. We made a ring from the change booth, and then, because two elderly, tight-lipped, nervous middle-aged women were entering the turnstile, Durkee grabbed my arm and hustled me through the exit doors calling thunderously to the agent: "I'm takin' my prisoner through now, Mac!" flashing his shield. And the two women stared with frozen faces, whispering excitedly as we marched down the platform. Our relief man departed on the same train with the women, and I caught a glimpse of them peering at us through the window with outraged faces.

Paul handed me a section of the paper and settled on the bench. I walked to the far end of the station and leaned against a pillar, feeling the dampness and coldness of the place. Outside, the air was crisp and fresh; here, the season was eternal. It made your bones ache with the unhealthy chill; the steel dust smudged your hands and face and clothing, and you couldn't take a deep breath without coughing.

For no reason, for no discernible reason, a feeling of anxiety was shooting through me: a roiling, uneven wave of uneasiness.

A train slid into the station. It was heralded by the low rumble far down the track, soft at first, then getting louder and filling the long cavern. The doors glided open and three people got out: a man and woman walking arm in arm and a tall, heavy-set Negro. He was about forty feet from me, almost in front of Durkee, who was on the bench. He stood for a moment, surveying the platform, watching the couple exit, then turned to watch the train pull away. He walked past Durkee to the other end of the station. He hadn't seen me. Durkee had his face down over his paper and was completely motionless. The man passed the bench again, walking lightly, tentatively seeking direction. I pressed hard against the pillar and could hear his feet moving closer. Then he stopped and began the descent, slowly, on the stairs of the passageway to the Independent subway.

I looked down the platform: the bench was empty. Somehow, invisibly, Durkee had gotten down the length of the platform and was behind me. He put his heavy hand on my shoulder. His eyes were shining with excitement, and he was looking toward the tunnel.

"Looks like our boy," he said, and we both knew he was right. We stood then at the top of the stairs and could hear a faint thudding sound. "He's prowling," Durkee said. "You go down first, I'll follow. I think he'll make the other side before we connect." He started me off so quickly I didn't have a chance to hesitate.

On the Independent platform, a train was just pulling out. No one had gotten off. Durkee waited on the landing, and I signaled for him to come up. The platform was empty. Durkee pulled me quickly to the edge of the platform—his instincts were incredible—and he gestured toward the far end of the station. The suspect was walking silently away from us; then he stopped, turned, stood motionless like some animal listening for danger, sniffing the air. Then he headed back toward us and the tunnel leading back to the BMT station. We flattened ourselves against the pillars at the farthest end of the platform and watched him enter the stairwell. He was walking more slowly now, descending the stairs with a purpose.

Durkee's voice, soft now, was surprisingly calm as we walked to the entrance of the tunnel. It was matter of fact, like this was something you do every day. "Now, I'm gonna have to be at least a staircase behind you—that's the setup—he sees me and that's it." His powerful hand was biting into my arm and his eyes, motionless for once, held mine. There was no question in his mind but that we were going into that tunnel, and I nodded. "Now, you're not gonna hear me and you're not gonna see me, but I'm gonna be there. You know that, don't you?" He spoke rapidly, exerting a slight pressure on my arm, leading me down the first step. I nodded again, and he winked and released me.

"Okay," I said. "I guess we go down." I stopped halfway down and looked back at him. He winked and grinned, and I held it in my mind and went ahead.

I could hear the sound of my shoes on the stairs. I had started to walk on my toes, then I remembered—I should be heard. The clicking step of a woman was being awaited somewhere within this winding passageway. I walked slowly, close to the wall on my left, so that I could take the corners. I had to give myself that much leeway against him—the waiter.

I walked down the three staircases and reached the bottom level and stopped, listening for the sounds of the suspect and also for the sounds of Durkee behind me. I heard nothing; I held my breath and felt my heart. I could taste that cold saliva that comes when you have been running fast in a cold wind or when you are fighting fear.

The landing was about twenty feet long and five feet wide; then there was a stairway leading up, to be followed by two other stairways and three corners to be turned. I had fully expected to be lunged at from some corner; the corners represented the danger, to my mind. There was a yellow bulb encased in wire beaming from the ceiling at the center of the stretch of landing, directly over a small water drain. A woman had been raped here, at this exact spot, two weeks ago.

I sensed his presence before I saw him, sensed the shadow at the top of the stairs, the flicker of movement not caused by the glare of the bulb. He was at the top of the stairs, waiting, listening for my hesitant step. I had my pocketbook in my left hand now, and I was leaning heavily against the right side of the passageway. The corners were on the other side now, and that was all I seemed to think about. I kept my eyes on the steps, concentrating on the slow, arduous, heavy climbing, and I saw his feet coming down the stairs along the left side of the staircase.

We were both walking slowly, and then we were passing each other, both on the same step, not touching, and it flashed through me, a kind of weightless relief, an instantaneous relaxation. He was past me, continuing on down the stairs. But he had whirled about and come behind me and was on the step below me. I could sense him though he had been soundless, sense the nearness before the impact of his body fell against me as he stood on the same step with me and grasped my throat with a hand encased in a leather glove. It was my first thought: he has a leather glove on his left hand. He pulled me back, close against him, and pressed something into my forehead and my eyes. Straining in the light I could see the shine of the revolver. It was silver.

His voice was hollow and warm in my ear: "Don't make a sound or I'll kill you! I'll pull the trigger!"

We stood unmoving then, and he pushed me with his shoulder. "Come up to this little landing here," he said, and somehow my feet complied, for I was climbing the steps and facing into the corner of dirty tile. He released my throat, his touch remaining—a scraping sensation—and he pulled me around to face him.

To say I was afraid would not be accurate. I felt a certain giddiness, a sense of unreality. Somehow, I had the feeling that this had all happened before—or rather, that it had been so intensely anticipated that it was almost a natural thing, a thing I had planned or was fully expecting. It was like being in a play, and we each had our words to say and our actions and our cues were determined. It wasn't a real occurrence; it was removed from any concrete reality.

We stood there confronting each other within the confines of the tile landing: it was as strange and desolate as a tomb. The quickening of all the processes of my own body, the sense of pounding, thudding, pulsating pressures, was reflected in his face. His heavy lips were parted and dry; his eyes, gleaming like startled points in the dim yellowness of the place, twitched. There was one incredible, breathless instant, a frozen moment in time, when neither of us moved or breathed, just regarded each other blankly, as though hypnotized, each by the other, not taking measure.

And then it snapped, that suspended time. My breath came in a painful, short spurt. The necessity to breathe brought us both back to the moment, but my mind, removed and apart from the numbness that was my body, made cold and clear observations. It was not paralyzed by the panic in my chest, the fear which buckled my knees weakly. My brain took control and frigidly ignored the contractions of my stomach. From some remote, safe, far, insane distance, my mind refused to admit any participation, refused to believe in its vulnerability, refused to recognize the brown, drawn face as Death's or the silver shining gun as the instrument of its eternity. Confronted with Death, that cool observer somewhere within me denied even the possibility of destruction and drew together all its faculties into a waiting and a watching. I knew, despite the hand that had grasped my throat, despite the revolver which had pressed against my forehead hard enough to leave its round imprint, I knew he could not destroy me. It was impossible.

My sense of observation seemed honed to a fantastic degree: the tiles behind him were clearly shaped, the yellow light on them created shadows and images. The man's face was sharply detailed: a small gutted scar on his cheek looked like a fat caterpillar, the stitch marks were furry and uneven. I could see the thick, short lashes on his eyes, the small, individual ovals of sweat around his mouth. I could smell fear surrounding us, heavy and thick as smoke, tangible and real, his fear as well as my own. My brain marked it, ignoring everything but this exact moment, discounting every other circumstance of my life or my experience. Only now, this moment, counted, meant anything. His eyes were the key to the man. They darted, twitched and flickered and gave him away.

"Whut you got in that pocketbook?" His husky voice was stretched thin and tight as a cord and was as hollow as air. And then it came to me: the advantage is mine. He doesn't know what I'm going to do, but I do.

I moved the pocketbook toward my body, my right

hand going to the clasp. His eyes dropped to follow the motion, and that was his mistake: failing to read my eyes. Fascinated by my hands, he did not see my right hand shoot out, directed by my brain, which said: Now! Now! I caught the inside of his right wrist, not hard, not very hard, but swiftly. Shocked, the hand lost its grip on the gun, which flew through the air and landed, clattering, on the stairway which stretched upward toward the next landing.

We lunged together then, but we were moving toward different goals—he was reaching upward to the top step where the gun lay, and I was clinging to his waist and feeling the strength of his body trying to shake me off. He gained his feet and thrust me from him without turning, but that sharp voice within said: Hold! Hold him! I became a part of him, of his feet, his knees, his thighs, his torso, holding him, weighing him down away from that gun, from climbing upward. I dragged him down, feeling the brutal scraping of the steel-edged cement steps on my legs, aware of the dark smell and feel of his corduroy jacket on my face, which was lost against him, my hands and arms blindly holding. We rose, then tumbled, both losing our footing. Then his weight was against me like a heavy blanket and we fell, and it came to me that our wrestling had been an almost silent thing—no sound but the soft grunts of breath and resolve.

For some curious reason my voice was inhibited by the immediate problem. What do you yell? Help? Come on? In the center of all this, then, was my awareness of myself, a crazy, wild, senseless awareness of myself, shattered suddenly by an explosion of sound, wordless, like a cry from an animal. I did not control or direct this cry, but I felt my prisoner edging from my hold, upward. Then Paul Durkee was there, over us, saying something and leaning heavily and untangling my arms, prying my locked fingers apart and forcing the man's hands behind him into handcuffs. Durkee seemed to fill the tunnel, his body hugely in motion, expertly attending to his job.

I walked to the top of the stairs and picked up the gun and held it, heavy and glistening, in the palm of my

hand. My brain believed it now, accepted it, as I felt the
heft of the weapon and touched its shape. I went down
the steps to where the prisoner lay face down, his body
stretched upward on the stairs. Paul was standing over
him, his revolver in his hand.

I stood over him, prisoner now truly, and called softly,
"Hey." He turned his body, and with vile fury I kicked
him just once with whatever energy was left. My foot
slammed his stomach and he caught his breath soundlessly,
his eyes not seeing me. Paul's head jerked up in some
surprise, his face a question, and I met his eyes steadily.

"Take it easy, tiger," he said softly. "Papa's here now."

And then all emotion left me, and I was as empty and
as unfeeling as Death. My face became set and blank,
my mask in place.

I called the squad commander from inside the change
booth. The agent, a small, hunched little man, gaped
wide-eyed at the prisoner leaning against the wall, feet
set back and forehead bearing his full weight, and at Durkee, holding his revolver close to the prisoner's head. The
squad commander let out one small whoop and said a
wagon would be on its way, and I hung up and lit a
cigarette. The agent, nervous and distraught, told me
smoking was prohibited in the station, but something in
my face must have reached him. He waved his hand and
laughed and said, "No, it's okay, it's okay, go ahead and
smoke."

The wagon came quickly, or it seemed to arrive quickly, and then we were entering the station house. The squad
commander was at the desk waiting, and several uniformed men were there, all waiting, watching Durkee lead
the prisoner up the stairs. The squad commander
stopped, turned and waited for me, then put his hand on
my shoulder. "Okay?" he said. "Are you okay, Mrs.
Uhnak?" I nodded and he hesitated a moment, then let
me pass him, and we entered the Detectives' Room. I
sat at the nearest vacant desk and held my hand over
the blotter: there was no tremor. Durkee had gone into
the squad commander's office, and a uniformed lieutenant entered the room, walked past me, and closed the

door to the squad commander's office behind him. I began writing in my cramped, backward little handwriting, consulting my watch, noting times and locations. I heard a phone ring and heard a detective's voice saying: "What the hell's the big deal—she's a policewoman, that's her job. Well, come over if you want. It's up to you." And then he hung up, cast a quick glance at me, met my face and must have seen something there. He shrugged. "These newspaper guys are going to be climbing all over you." But I didn't answer and he walked back to his own desk.

The activity was all around me. Detectives issued back and forth from the squad commander's office to their complaint file box. They were pulling out slips of paper and calling complainants to come down to the precinct or court the next morning to make a positive identification. I felt possessed by some terrible calmness, some lack of feeling, as though I were invisible, sitting here in the midst of all this activity and excitement and phone-calling, having no part in it—it not concerning me in any way. I felt like some intruder who had wandered into this place and would be asked to leave as soon as someone noticed me.

There was a detective at a desk by the door, scrawling on his note pad, nodding. Then he looked up at me, and his hand missed placing the phone on its receiver. He lit a cigarette, his eyes on me all the time, then finally came over.

"I'm O'Calin," he said, and it surprised me. He looked Italian. He was regarding me with some strange curiosity. "Are you okay?" he asked, but with a lack of concern.

"I'm fine."

"You want something—a shot or something?"

"No."

His voice was harsh and unfriendly. "You're pretty cool, aren't you?" It was a contemptuous compliment.

I looked at him fully now. He was studying me, looking for some reaction. "I'm an iceberg," I said, feeling that cold and that lifeless. He blinked at me, slid his eyes over me, sucked his cheek and walked away.

I could hear the voices now, Durkee's, the squad commander's, some other detectives'. Then, suddenly, the door burst open and Durkee barreled out.

"What the hell are you doing here?" he roared. "They're in there slicing up the pie—getting the pinches lined up. Don't you want your slice?"

I saw O'Calin watching me. "Yes," I said, and let Durkee half push me into the squad commander's office.

Apparently, my presence was strictly Durkee's idea. The squad commander, a thin, balding man with watery blue eyes, looked up from his desk, and they all looked up at me as though I were some apparition; but I was no intruder there. It came to me then. I was *supposed* to be there. I looked around, counting them—the prisoner, cuffed by each hand to a chair before the desk, some unknown detectives seated on either side of him, and the uniformed lieutenant leaning against a file cabinet, and two other detectives standing by the window. Durkee grabbed an empty chair and pulled it up alongside his and motioned me into it. I sat down and no one said a word. The squad commander coughed, glanced at some papers on his desk, and resumed the interrogation as though I hadn't interrupted.

The prisoner, his head down, answered in grunts, acknowledging all the accusations: Yeah, yeah, yeah. That was me. Yeah, that was me, too. Yeah. He acknowledged the stacks of pawn tickets on the desk which had been taken from his pockets: jewelry, rings, watches. Yeah, he pawned them. Yeah, he took them from those women. Yeah.

O'Calin entered and tapped on the door at the same time and said to the squad commander: "Reporters from the *News* and *Mirror*. They wanna talk to the policewoman." The watery eyes slid to me. "You ready to talk to them?"

"Yes," I said. "I'm ready to talk to them."

My voice, telling it, was steady and even in answer to their questions, and I volunteered nothing. I just told them what they wanted to know, flatly, methodically, the way you write the reports up—a cold, routine police event. Then the questions stopped, and I noticed a phone was free. I picked it up and asked for an outside line. Tony picked the phone up on the first ring and wasn't surprised to hear from me.

"We got him," I said, "the Fulton Street mugger. He held a gun on me. I guess I did a stupid thing—knocked it from his hand. No, I'm okay, truly, Honey. Just tired, you know."

Telling him, telling Tony, it was a completed thing now; whatever else was to come, this part of it was completed. His voice was a whisper; I hated the sound of it —the worry and the concern—and I wanted to be with him now. We spoke for a moment, and I asked him to call my mother and my sister to say I was all right— not a scratch. "You're too calm," he said, catching it, knowing my defense. "Ask someone to give you a drink or something."

"No," I said, "not yet. I need this—you know that I need this right now." And he said yes and reluctantly ended the conversation. And then I looked up, and there were the reporters, grinning, taking their notes. They had recorded my end of the conversation.

The director of the Policewomen's Bureau arrived shortly after that, but the reporters were gone by then. Her face was unreadable and her voice steady and even. "Are you all right, Mrs. Uhnak?"

"Yes, I'm fine."

And then, coldly, "Was this the only way you could have taken him?"

"No," I said quietly. "I was grandstanding."

She snapped away from me, wordless, and entered the squad commander's office. Then they all came out, the prisoner between Durkee and another detective, and she came up to me. "You're taking the pinch—assault, attempted robbery and 1897. The others are dividing up the various other arrests as soon as they get identification from the other complainants. After the arraignment to-morrow, I want to see you in my office." And then she was gone.

Photographers were downstairs now, and they flashed their lights at us, aiming at me, placing me next to the giant of a prisoner, telling us look here, look up at him, come on, kid, put your head way back, he's a big one. The prisoner was booked, and then the squad commander said to me, "Durkee and O'Calin and Davis are taking him to his place—we want a search of his belongings to see if anything else turns up. You want to go?"

"Yes," I said. "I want to go."

I don't know why I went: maybe just so I wouldn't get squeezed out, maybe just to finish with it all the way.

A Brooklyn slum is like any other slum and a Brooklyn tenement is like any other tenement and a Negro ghetto is like any other Negro ghetto. Durkee took my arm as we trailed the others. "Don't touch the walls," he said. "Roaches."

They pounded on the door, and a small, thin, dark girl, her eyes wide and black, stood back, wordlessly, and let us all enter. She didn't look at the prisoner, Thomas Anderson, age 22, male, Negro, born U.S. She was neither surprised nor excited nor upset, but leaned silently against a wall, watching, not really seeing. Her husband sat on the edge of a low chair, its broken upholstery showing cottony gaps. The place was a series of tiny rooms that were wider than they were long. There was a separate boxlike kitchen, with a bathtub taking up one wall. There were pots and dishes everywhere, and four big black cockroaches were scrambling up the side of the old-fashioned refrigerator. Durkee pointed and pulled me back. The girl, no more than seventeen, came into the kitchen. She was swollen with child, her face puffy with that mask of expectation.

They had told her they were looking for jewelry or pawn tickets. "Did he ever give you things like that?" Durkee asked. "Presents?"

"The only thing he ever give me was this," she answered, looking down at her body and resting her folded arms on its round fullness.

The other detective, Davis, came into the kitchen. "You got two TV sets, Mrs. Anderson, huh?"

"Yeah," she said, "and owe on both of them."

They went around the place collecting tickets, a few

odd pieces of jewelry, a cheap watch, a costume pin. Durkee went into the darkness of the other room and then we were alone, the girl and I, and she was motionless and unquestioning. She hadn't even asked what her husband had done.

"When are you going to have the baby?" I asked.

She jerked one shoulder. "I dunno."

"Well, have you made any arrangements? I mean, what hospital will you go to?"

She shrugged again. "I dunno."

Her eyes were round and large and showed the fear that her blank, young, loose features had concealed. A moment passed, was shared, and I wanted to say something to her. "Look," I said weakly, for it had no meaning. "Look, I'm sorry." About what, I don't know. About her husband, sure to get at least twenty years; about her baby, to be born somewhere, sometime soon, to be returned to this hovel, these dark and filthy and ratty rooms. But that's what I said, and the girl pushed out her lip and narrowed her eyes suspiciously.

"Whut you care?" she asked. "Whut's it mean to you?"

You're right: it doesn't mean a damn thing to me, not any of it, none of it, not you or your husband or your child or your life. It has nothing to do with me. And I will forget you and your swollen body and his eyes and twitching face and my own coldness, and none of this can touch me, because I am as cold as ice and incapable of being touched. Not by you or any of them. I am hard as stone and devoid of feeling, because this is how you have to be: this is your only defense.

9

"You have become famous and your face is known"

I will never believe anything I read in the newspapers or hear on radio or see in the so-called news broadcasts on television. I know that it is all a game and that they take a person and shape and define and manipulate that person into whatever form or dimension suits the immediate needs or purposes of the media. I know that an event is plastic and that truth as extended to the public is lurking somewhere between all the words. I know this because it was done to me. There was a lull in sensational news at the time I apprehended the mugger of Fulton Street, and so the case was headlined and featured for as many days as it could be milked and stretched —until the next outline of an event came along to replace my exploits and my public image.

The director of policewomen informed me, in her office, that I was to be promoted to detective third grade. I was surprised, because departmental policy dictates against what is called "on-the-spot" promotions, for what I believe is a good reason. A sudden, single act of good police work is often performed by an officer at a moment of confrontation, but this does not necessarily indicate that the officer should be promoted; it is often a fluke. I went through the ceremonies at City Hall, seeing the mayor and the police commissioner and the collected crowds in the same kind of unnatural calmness that had gripped me through the days following the arrest of Anderson. It was only later, at home, holding the coveted "gold shield" in the palm of my hand, that I began to feel any real emotions.

"I deserved this shield," I said to Tony, who smiled.

145

"Of course you did," he said.

"No." I shook my head. "That isn't what I mean. I deserved it before this. This is a 'headline shield'—a forced promotion. They didn't have any choice. They should have given it to me months ago on the basis of my past work. My record is good. I have enough pinches and convictions to have merited this a long time ago. I wouldn't have gotten this promotion if it hadn't been for all the publicity."

To pacify me, he said that it didn't matter: I *did* get the promotion, and the Honorable Mention Award which entitled me to membership in the Police Honor Legion. It was the highest honor a police officer could attain.

I saw my picture on the front pages of the morning papers and in the second section of the afternoon papers: a smiling girl confidently holding onto the arm of the large, dark prisoner; a grinning policewoman saluting the mayor, regarding the new detective shield with pride. It was all false. All the words written by the featured columnists and the lighthearted admiration of three editors of the city's biggest newspapers: JUST ROUTINE, SAYS LITTLE LADY COP! DOROTHY'S LITTLE, BUT OH MY! NEVER UNDERESTIMATE THE POWER OF A WOMAN! They told the story of the assignment, shifting the facts and details around for greater interest, describing my astonishing feats of judo: "Dorothy tossed the amazed Anderson with a combination of three basic judo holds [and they had pictures of me demonstrating, as I had been told to do] and flattened him with a karate slash; had him handcuffed and half unconscious to be delivered to her admiring partner." And there was a picture of my admiring partner, his eyes popping, regarding me wildly, as I regarded the camera with a wooden grin.

I sat with the newspaper men, each in turn, each entitled according to the police department's public relations department to an exclusive interview, and I answered the questions coolly and carefully. I had been briefed and instructed. Not exactly warned and admonished, but the sharp, shrewd eyes of the director of policewomen sensed some vague and resentful stubbornness in my silence at her instructions.

"You understand, of course, Mrs. Uhnak," she intoned, "that in giving these interviews you are the spokesman for 250 policewomen. Your words are our words, and this is a heavy responsibility."

So I was told: Don't be yourself; you are to be the image of us. It was that about it all that I felt most heavily. You stop being an individual. You have no personal identity. To have said, "Yes, I was afraid. I was as scared as any woman would be under the circumstances," would have been to negate the public image of the police. We must remain inhuman and separate and apart, another species. Facing death is no more than a routine thing which we were trained and paid to do.

The television shows were worse, much worse. I was sent to two early morning news broadcasts. I had to arrive at one studio in the dark of night, though it was five-thirty in the morning. I sat and watched this man, tall and smooth and grinning at an hour when any normal man would still be pulling the covers over his head. He ran through his scheduled joviality and introduced a group of ten short, muscular, inarticulate young wrestlers from an assorted collection of country-wide boys' clubs; they were in New York to compete at some show at Madison Square Garden. These Neanderthal little runts sputtered and stammered and hitched up their pants and made their tough little monkey faces into the camera, the color draining from their faces, as the M.C. feigned fright at their potential strength. And during the pre-broadcast run-through, sitting on the side, I listened to an immaculately groomed social arbitrator, some elegant man who had written various books about the inside of upper society, as he regaled me with what he considered fascinatingly offbeat material about names with hyphens that meant nothing to me. Then he raised his handsome arched eyebrows and, as if in afterthought, asked me who I was, seeking my right or reason for sharing this stage with him. I was obviously not a member of that little group of wary young musclemen. It stuck in my throat. I murmured that I was a policewoman, and he drew back slightly. "Good heavens," he said, not quite knowing how to cope with this bit of information. "And what have you done?" Apparently, I had not made the society page.

I shrugged slightly. "Nothing much, this is just an assignment," and his interest, which had been migratory, waned as he launched into some story about third-rate royalty and Palm Beach.

The show was taped, and after his portion of it, he wiped his forehead and whispered to me, "As soon as it's run off, I have to call my wife; she'll tell me how I did. Listen, how did it seem to you?" It struck me as odd that he was looking for some sort of acceptance from me—perhaps he was just democratic at heart.

When I was interviewed, the man running the show, a sweet-faced fellow with a Midwestern accent who kept calling me "Dor'thy," kept shaking his head. At one point he actually reached out to squeeze my muscle.

"My goodness, Dor'thy," he gushed, "you seem so little," as though I were shrinking down before his eyes. He made me stand up to his six-foot-three inches of lank and bone, and I spoke in a flat, monotonous litany, telling my story by rote. He kept trying to liven it up with gasps and groans and "my goodnesses" at every pause, and I felt a little sorry for him. We waited until the show was run off, watching it on the monitor, and the social expert ran and made his call, then came back, slightly agitated.

"My wife," he said accusingly, "said that you came over much better than I did. She said I fidget. Heavens, I never knew I was fidgeting. Did you detect any fidgets?" I told him no, but he took no comfort from this. Then the group of wrestlers, eying me like some future or ancient enemy, grunted their good-bys, jerking their hands at us. The long, cold, immaculate fingers of the society man slithered into my hand, and he looked beyond me and bade me good luck. I think I had spoiled his day because I hadn't fidgeted.

My next appearance was on a woman's daytime TV show, and Paul Durkee was to appear with me for a joint interview. It was one of those quiz shows. They had a wheel that spun around, and when it stopped a typewritten question on a subject of the wheel's choosing popped out. The M.C. was one of those perpetually beaming men; he had a forced, happy face, but there were networks of red veins around his short, snub nose. There was a tremor in his hands and he had bleary eyes. He winced at Paul's boisterous voice and wide gestures. His name was "Smiling" Somebody-or-other, and he kept smiling all the time when anybody could see he just wanted to put his head down somewhere and sleep it off.

He was openly concerned about Durkee, for Paul was hamming it up, interrupting the pre-broadcast briefing with loud noises and lapses into the kind of language that would make anybody stop smiling.

"Now," he said, "we'll talk about your experience for about five minutes. I think we'll let Dorothy tell the story, and then, Paul," he said with that easy familiarity of his profession, "you can add some comments. . . ."

"You bet I will," Paul said. "I wanna tell you this kid really knocked 'em dead. Why she . . ."

The smile was painful but still in evidence. "Yes, fine. We'll run through it in its entirety before air time. And then we'll ask Dorothy the four big jackpot questions, and if she gets them all right, we'll ask her the big jackpot super question."

I felt panic: all this buildup and then I'd probably goof on those questions. It was the way I felt, but some other man, some assistant to somebody, kept poking at me and winking. Paul hauled him off into some corner and was in fierce conversation with him.

"Don't worry, kiddo," Paul said, just loudly enough to be heard by the M.C. "The whole show is fixed—they're gonna give you the answers before we get on."

Mr. Smiling kept his face buried in his notes. Four different members of the program approached me, each whispering "test questions" at me, and we ran through the whole thing and then we were on TV.

I sat in the hard plastic chair and told my story, and Paul reinforced it with frequent interruptions, waving his arms around and rolling his eyes, which searched frantically for the right camera. The M.C. kept interrupting Paul, his mind on the signals he was getting from some man behind the camera who kept rolling his hands for us to hurry up. There was a lot of applause and admiring groans from the audience of plump little out-of-town housewives with nothing better to do with their afternoon. Then Mr. Smiling, cutting Paul off with a blinding smile, got up and sang a little song to me in his thin, shaky, daytime TV voice. I stood there feeling like some kind of idiot. It is a very unnerving thing to have a man sing right at you in public; you don't know what to do with your hands or where to look. I kept staring at his mouth. I could see the nicotine stains on his teeth, and I could hear Paul pounding time with his feet. Then the song was over and there was a tinny flourish of trumpets. I was marched over to the wheel and I spun it and proceeded to answer the four questions. Of course they were the "test questions," and I responded with the answers I had been given. Mr. Smiling stamped his feet and had the audience whoop it up for me each time. I could feel my face burning and my smile frozen on my mouth. Paul roared out over everybody else, "Isn't she terrific!" and his face was bunched up into a look of such sincerity that the camera focused on him. That only led him to further utterances; he was having a wonderful time, laughing right in their faces and they thought he was on the level.

I missed the super-super jackpot question and so lost a trip to Spain and a dishwasher: no one had cued me on this one. For one terrible moment, both Mr. Smiling and I thought Paul was going to make a scene about that, but he just sat there, making faces and wiping his hands all over his eyes and the audience moaned in sympathy. Paul was having the time of his life. I ended up with a grand total of $250, which Paul and I were to split between us, and a box of hair lotion and powdered detergent and menthol cigarettes and some cold tablets.

They practically had to drag Paul off the stage to make way for the next contestants, and the M.C. looked like he needed a shot to get him through the rest of the show.

Some assistant producer said he'd mail the check to me in a few days, and that I should split with Paul. I gave Paul the cartons of menthol cigarettes, and he held them in his large hands as if they were contaminated. He looked around wildly for a wastebasket, then hurled the cartons of cigarettes from him as if they were burning his fingers.

The assistant producer gasped in horror and retrieved the cartons, clutching them to him like children. He moved his head around quickly and spoke in a whisper: "Jesus Christ, the sponsor is around—you want to get us canned?"

Paul started to make a speech about the sponsor, but I took his arm and led him to the door. He stopped on the stairway and said, in a calm, rational, perfectly sane voice, "Wasn't that a nutty ball? My God, what screwballs in this world!"

That night, I received a phone call from some woman with the artificial tones of hurriedly acquired culture. She told me how proud the people of New York were of me, and how delighted they would be to have me as a guest on their well-known, coast-to-coast evening musical quiz show at the end of the week. It was a very big money show. You had to run across the stage in your stocking feet and ring a bell before your opponent did and then identify the song the orchestra was playing. Then you had to answer questions on a medley of songs and keep coming back every week until you had amassed a fortune.

"So, my dear, we'd like you to come down tomorrow morning for a briefing; we've cleared it, of course, with the police department."

"No," I said quietly, "I'm afraid I can't."

"But you don't understand, dear. I've spoken to Inspector Rodgers at Public Relations, and he gave me your phone number. So it's all set."

"No," I said. "I don't want to be on your show. I'm too tired. I have an ulcer and my doctor said to take it easy: no more strain; no more TV. No more any of this."

The voice was brittle but still bright and certain. "Our prize money, dear, is quite high, as I'm sure you know."

"I'm not interested. Besides, I don't know anything at all about music—I'm completely tone deaf."

The laugh in my ear was wise and knowing and seemed relieved to have hit on the real problem. "You won't have to worry about that, my dear. Good heavens, don't worry about that at all. We'll have a little . . . briefing . . . you know." She spoke archly and, she thought, discreetly.

I had just wanted to hear her say it, but I was really too tired to care any more. "No. I don't want to run across your lousy stage in my stocking feet and ring your lousy bell and win your lousy money."

Now the voice was shocked, hurt and outraged. "Now just a minute. Do you realize that we have a waiting list of contestants from all over the country? Do you realize that it's a privilege to appear on our show? Do you realize that *hardly anyone* can *get on our show?*"

"Good," I said. "Call someone up from your big endless list and give them my place." And I hung up.

There were other phone calls: crank calls from any nut with a dime and a phonebook, strange hollow voices rising with some peculiar excitement, starting out with a compliment on my work and ending in obscenities. And friends—well meaning but also touched with some curious excitement for detail. Finally, Tony said he would have the phone company change our number, and it would remain unlisted. We kept the phone off the hook after eight o'clock at night.

I went to see the director of policewomen the next morning. "I turned down that music show because I'm sick. My ulcer has been acting up and my doctor has put me on medication which is slowing me down. I'm sorry, but I just don't think I can do any more of these shows."

"Do you want to go on sick leave?" she asked quietly.

"No, ma'am. I just don't want to go on any more television shows."

"I see. Of course you realize all these assignments were purely voluntary." I didn't argue. I nodded. "Let's see now: you were on three television shows and two radio interviews, yes? Very well, Mrs. Uhnak. Report to the Bureau tomorrow morning and we'll see about your new assignment." She studied her long white nails for a moment. "As you may know, there is a bit of difficulty relative to your new assignment."

I must have looked surprised, for she continued, nodding her head. "Yes, I'm not too sure where we're going to place you. You see," she was studying me now, curiously looking for something in my face, "you have become rather well known. Many of the squads that use women detectives are," she searched for a word, " 'wary,' I guess you'd say, of someone who has been so much in the public eye."

"Really?" My voice was shaky and tense. "Do the squad commanders think I'm some kind of prima donna? Do they think that all this publicity was for *me?*"

Her eyes glinted and her voice was harsh. "I am not questioning their motives," and then she added, meanly, "or yours. I am merely relaying this information to you. You are a little too hot right now."

"A hot shot maybe?"

"Well, that would be for you to say, wouldn't it?" We sat watching each other, neither of us moving an inch, neither of us showing anything, revealing anything. Finally, she broke the silence with a sigh, moved her hands on her desk. "Mrs. Uhnak, I seriously suggest you take a day or two off. You have some overtime coming. Why don't you just relax at home and let me work this out?" If there was some kindness in her voice, just some hint of concern, her face concealed it. Yet I felt there was some great burden on her; there was some strangely indefinable sympathy between us and it was not the director I should be fighting.

"Yes. I'm sorry. It's just that it's been too much—all this running around. I don't feel well and I'm tired."

An open bid for sympathy was the wrong tactic, and there was to be no camaraderie. Her face hardened and she nodded. "Very well, you may have the next two tours off. Fill out the o.t. sheets and I'll sign them, and you may be excused for the rest of today as well." And then she became busy with her own work.

Tony and I sat that night and watched my image on a

rerun of a news broadcast. There I was, smiling without much expression, speaking in that intolerably quiet, self-assured voice: the voice of the college actress, measuring out the pauses, sluffing off the dangers, speaking it all and marking it all as "routine"—underplaying it for effect, the excitement of the commentator heightened by my own offhand and calculated manner.

I watched the girl in the picture, appearing for barely three minutes, telling it all casually and unremarkably. "It's all so phony," I said. It wasn't like that—none of it was like that. Not one of them asked me what it was *really* like." The words came finally, in a torrent of sound and feeling. We had both been waiting it out, both knew it had to burst so that I could be free of it. I gasped and choked over all of it and Tony sat, pressing my hands inside of his, not trying to stop me. "There was that one terrible moment: just the two of us and nothing else in the world was real, and all our lives, everything either one of us had done up to that second, counted for nothing. And we just stood there, facing each other, and everything in our futures depended on each other, like we were the only two people in the entire world and everything was right there, in that rotten, damp, flickering tunnel. In my whole life, no one was ever as important as *he* was then." I stopped, seeing Tony's face through the wet tears that streaked my eyes. "Can you understand that? Just that man and me, and both of our lives were, were *encased* there, by those tile walls; everything began and ended right there. I thought about it—it actually flashed through me that only he and I were there. That big dark face, sweaty and panting, and me, like I was some stranger in my own body. We were so completely alone and I can't help wondering what *he* felt—I mean, I know what he is . . . I know what he's done . . . all those poor women . . . I've met them in court and spoken to them and seen them cry, and their husbands have held my hands . . . but I can't help wondering what *he* feels now. He was there too. He went through exactly what I went through and they're trading on it, on the destruction o someone's life. If I had been killed, they would have interviewed him in the police station and they'd be asking you for old snapshots of me for their stories, and it would have all been the same—all of it. Maybe even a better story!"

I leaned against Tony's shoulder and let the sobs shake me, not fighting it any more, forcing words out spasmodically, trying to get it all out, snuffling wetly. "And they look at me like I'm some kind of freak—they admire me and make a big fuss. They hold me up like I'm something in a glass case and keep asking me, How did you feel? At the moment when he held the gun on you, how did you feel? God, God, how do they think I felt? And that stupid girl on television, simpering and shrugging. 'It was my job; after all, I'm a policewoman and that was my assignment.' What do they know about it? What do any of them know about it?"

And then, finally, I put the other part of it into words: "And that poor, miserable pregnant girl—his wife—in that filthy place and with a child going to be born and his father in prison for all his growing years. Another one for us; give him twelve or fifteen years and he'll be right out there. And that girl, saying to me, 'What do you care? What are we to you?' And I didn't answer her, I didn't say anything, because I told myself she was right."

Tony pulled me back and tilted my face up to his. "And was she right?"

I shook my head. "No. She was wrong. Or maybe I'm wrong, because *I care*. God Almighty, what's wrong with me? Do I have to care about everybody and everything? Do I have to see their lives?"

The check came the next morning and I cashed it and I counted out the money in the crisp new tens and twenties. I counted out one hundred and twenty-five dollars into two neat stacks. Then I bought an envelope and a stamp at the stationery store and put one of the stacks of money into the envelope and wrote Mrs. Anderson's name on it and her address and nothing else, and sealed and stamped it. I put Paul's share in my pocketbook. Then

I dropped the envelope into the mail box and clinked the lid twice to make sure it fell inside.

And I wondered, walking home, exactly what it was that I was trying to buy for one hundred and twenty-five dollars.

10

"Oh, read my future brightly;
oh, make it all come true"

The Police Department does not persist with its heroes; there is not a gradual letting go. It is a quick thing, as quick as the event. One day your name is headlined, editorialized; your picture is on the front pages and on the television screens—and the next day you are on patrol. You are even, to some degree, suspect. Should you follow up a sensationalized arrest with another unusual incident, eyebrows are raised, voices are lowered and suspicions are voiced. On the other hand, should your arrest record hit a slump, questions are raised as to whether or not you are resting on your laurels. Publicity marks you in the Department, and you are aware of being watched and studied. Future partners regard your reaction to your celebrity. If you are too casual about it—"Who does she think she's kidding?" If you openly enjoy and revel in it —"What a swell-headed hot shot!"

My "public relations" role for the Department lasted some two weeks, and then I was assigned, temporarily, to the Bureau of Special Services. It is—to my mind—the "elite squad," the dream squad. These are the men and women who draw the most interesting assignments in the Department. They guard and accompany the President and his family on visits to New York, accompany visiting royalty or heads of government. Though they work fantastic hours and bear tremendous responsibility, they also have great opportunities to meet and mingle with not just "important" people, but dynamic, interesting people one does not ordinarily come to know. Chosen because of their personalities and abilities not only as police officers but as informed, competent people, many of the detectives

157

in this squad are bilingual. Of course, working with internationally known personalities is not their major assignment. Special Services also handles undercover assignments, checks on organizations that might be subversive or questionable, keeps abreast of labor problems to keep the Department alerted to any emergency conditions. There are only four or five women assigned permanently to B.O.S.S., and I was sent to fill in for one of the women who had broken her leg in a skiing mishap upstate. I arrived dreaming of queens and kings.

My partner was a man named Charlie Hvolka, and he told me we were to conduct an investigation involving gypsies.

Most people associate fortune tellers with fairs or romantic songs, a kind of "fun thing" you go along with as part of a late summer afternoon's pleasure. The fortune tellers are part of that mysterious tribe called "gypsies," whose origins are lost and unknown, and therefore, to the extender of the palm, all the more exotic. When I was about sixteen, my sister and I, along with two of her giggling friends, went to a tearoom, one of those bare, slightly shoddy rooms located up a flight of stairs over a "going-out-of-business" specialty shop somehow wedged between two glossy Fifth Avenue stores. The dirtiness of the stairs and the darkness of the hallway added to our sense of excitement, though truly nothing is needed to add to the exhilaration of four teen-age girls about to have the world unfolded to them from the depths of their own hands.

One of my sister's friends, Miki, went first into a small area of the room cloaked off with shiny drapes of many colors. She glanced over at us as she entered the domain of the all-knowing Rahmajee. He was all-knowing because the small sign over the entry to his secret lair said so. She emerged shiny-eyed and slightly dazed ten minutes later, shaking her head at our questions, unable to speak of it. Not yet. Not yet. Waiting for my sister, I sipped the lukewarm tea, swallowing several bitter grains. The other girl, whoever she was I do not remember, told me not to disturb the cup as our fortunes and future were there, among the leaves. My turn came last (as befits the youngest), and I sat across a card table from a man of undetermined ancestry, marked "Indian" by a twist of grayish-white material wrapped around his head. His eyes were bright black, and a light from somewhere behind my head shone directly on his face, which glistened with some greasy substance. His voice was velvet-smooth and melodic, and he pressed his fingertips rhythmically on my outstretched fingers, tips on tips, slightest of pressures. He was getting the measure of my life and dreams and hopes and ambitions. Then he read my fortune, carefully choosing his words so that later, when we girls compared notes, there would be some variation, and we would know he had told each of us our true destiny. The words the dark man spoke are lost in time, but it would not be difficult to imagine what one would say to a breathless sixteen-year-old who has yet to discover the world: love, fame, misfortune, courage, eventual triumph. All there, in that marvelous hand, unlike any other hand ever created through all time, in all the universe.

And then I carried my cup of soggy tea leaves to a corner table, where some incredibly old woman hunched over them, scattering them on a saucer before her. Without looking at me, she read them so softly and in so strange an accent that to this day I do not know what my life was to be. I leaned forward just once to catch her words, but the hot foul breath was not worth the stream of mumbled words.

This, then, is usually the extent of our knowledge of gypsies and fortune tellers: a kind of fond, even thrilling memory of days when we were anxious and willing to accept a dream uniquely our own, and carry it around like a strange secret inside ourselves.

But there is more to it, for any police department in any large city has its stories about gypsies, and they are neither romantic nor funny.

Charlie Hvolka was a soft-spoken man of medium height and build, which is probably about two inches shorter than he'd like to be and about ten pounds heavier. He had a round, mild face and high broad cheek bones, small eyes and dry-looking lips; his voice was very soft and careful, because he spoke many languages and was aware of occasionally slipping into the accents of his childhood Russian. There was no telltale hardness in Charlie's face, and if asked to guess his occupation, you'd probably have said he was a schoolteacher, professor or librarian, or one of those tiptoe-walking multitudes who wordlessly provide some service for you without intruding their features on your memory. This was one of Charlie's strongest assets; the only part of him that was pure policeman was his mind, and that was made of hard spikes of metal that clicked quickly and missed nothing.

"We have received information," Charlie said, using the professional police way of saying that he was not going to tell me anything of the background of the case, "that this woman, a Madame Zoruba, is a steerer for an abortionist. She is a shrewd old witch, and we haven't been able to get anything definite on her. She speaks Polish mostly, but she can speak and understand English. She has this place set up on the upper West Side, and it's a kind of 'temple' or something, a 'church.' She does some fortunetelling, but her gimmick is that it's not for money: you make a 'contribution' to her church."

Madame Zoruba was not a swindler who practiced separating middle-aged, greedy women from their newly acquired widow's gold. This is a fairly common operation, made possible by an incredible awareness of human avarice. I had worked on some of these cases when I was in the Policewomen's Bureau. Various switches are pulled on the victim, handkerchiefs are placed around money, chickens are strangled in paper bags, curses are declared to be present, evil money must be cleansed. And they go along with it, these middle-aged women who are more numerous and generally more intelligent than can be believed. They are in quest of wealth promised them by the swindling gypsy who, of course, is the only one to gain by the various transactions. They are patient, the gypsies, waiting sometimes for months before actually confiscating the money, during which interval the victim tells herself that it must be true, it must be real. If it were a fraud, the gypsy would have taken the money. But she held it for weeks, and the taint is still on it, and she gave it back to me. I will bring her the chicken and if the chicken dies in the bag with the money, we will know it is cursed, and she shall cleanse it for me and then it will multiply, like she said, three times! They are patient, the swindlers, but for their own reasons. The victim loses all sense of time: how many meetings, what transpired, when the money actually slipped from her possession. And when the hysterical woman appears, shamefaced and horror-stricken at the district attorney's office, her story is garbled, inaccurate, and all she knows is that somewhere along the line her fifteen thousand dollars of insurance money disappeared. The chances of building a case against the swindler are negligible, more often than not, impossible.

Unfortunately, too often the police *know* that a crime has transpired, who the criminal is and how the victim was victimized, but are powerless to do anything about it. The law is specific, and of necessity must protect the innocent. But in the course of such protection it spreads a warm blanket of immunity around many criminals. The policeman wants one thing in a case against a criminal: get him right—with enough evidence for a conviction. It's the only way to get him: right.

Madame Zoruba had not been gotten, though she had gotten away with many things. There was no real evidence against her: just knowledge that she was, among other things, a steerer for an abortionist. This abortionist was also known "on information." What we wanted was an air-tight case.

Charlie Hvolka briefed me, and we began to study our roles as intently as actors. A major part of the life of any detective, doing any kind of undercover work, is the ability to assume a new identity. The detective must not play-act, but he must live his new role, believe it, under whatever circumstances he finds himself.

"You must *be* this girl," Charlie explained. "You must become this girl of Polish descent, and remember that you grew up in that orphanage upstate, which is why you do not speak Polish. You *look* Polish with your fair hair and light eyes. You have to *feel* your Polish blood."

I didn't know what it meant to feel Polish, but I started "thinking Polish," watching Charlie's face, his gestures as he walked about the small office speaking in the language to me, gesturing, surrounding me with what he called "the air of it," giving me an understanding of the feeling, a kind of instant "Polish-ization."

"No one can catch you in a lie when you are being someone else, because you have no real background: you make it up as you need to, and they can't trip you up because none of it is real, so all of it is real."

It sounded, at first, like double-talk, but as we worked it out, the girl started to grow, to become real, to become me, or I to become her. I started to feel a sadness, a self-pity for the bitterness and emptiness of my life as we talked. Charlie threw questions at me—not giving me the answers. Find them for yourself, it's your life, not mine. I will believe what you tell me if *you* believe it is true.

"Don't say too much," he cautioned. "The less you say, the less you have to remember, and the less you have to remember, the less chance you have of getting tripped up on your own words. It all comes from you—whatever they will know of you comes only from you, because you will tell it."

And so, after a week, I was Helen Wroblewski, twenty-three years old; salesgirl in the five-and-ten on Broadway and 45th Street; single; pregnant; wronged by Charlie who was married and twenty years older than me and was section manager in my five-and-ten. But he was kind to me, trying to help me, willing to go along with me. My friend Mary Rosinski, at the cosmetic counter, told me to go see Madame Zoruba because a friend of a friend's cousin said, "Go and see Madame Zoruba when you got that kind of trouble."

"Now if she makes us," Charlie said, "we let it go; we don't press anything. I don't think you look like a cop and you don't think I look like a cop, but she might think we both have shields on our foreheads. We just play it by ear and see what happens."

Madame Zoruba's was not a typical gypsy storefront opening on the street. It was down about six steps, in the basement of a shoddy, once elegant brownstone on West 93rd Street. There was an iron grating over the entrance-way, which was located beneath the stairway to the first floor of the building. There was a small sign over the bell and a larger one of chipped black paint on the door. MADAME ZORUBA, the signs said, and over the letters was a faded yellow symbol of a crescent moon and five-pointed stars. We rang the bell a second time, and when the door opened, Charlie had his hand on my shoulder. In the darkness of the doorway, Madame Zoruba looked us over quickly, then said something to Charlie in Polish.

Charlie spoke hesitantly, and I gathered she was asking us who we were, what we wanted of her. They spoke for at least two minutes, and I would not meet her eyes, which were studying me. Finally, she jutted her chin decisively at me as Charlie, facing me now, explained me. Then she opened the door and let us walk past her, to grope in the darkened entrance hall. She grunted some direction to us, and Charlie parted the hanging beads which covered an archway into a small, hot room which was filled in every corner by ancient, worn, velvet-covered furniture—a great stuffed sofa, three armchairs, a foot-rest as large as an easy-chair. The original color had probably been some shade of green, but it was grayish now, and there were traces here and there of some gold fringe along the bottoms. There were tables placed wher-ever a chair ended, and massive, ugly lamps, all unlit, were on every table. There were pictures hung haphazard-ly on the walls up to the low, chipped ceiling: dark brown photographs of dark old people staring out blankly at some ancient camera.

Seen in the dreary dimness of the room, Madame Zoru-ba strikingly resembled the furnishings with which she had surrounded herself. She was a short, heavy woman, upholstered in an endless series of nondescript skirts topped off with a thick blouse of heavy, cheap satin, which had apparently been white at some long forgotten time. She was like some animated junk-jewelry shop. She clinked and rattled and clanged from all manner of hanging things (long, beaded metallic loops of things hung from about her neck, dull beads and tarnished chains with dangling amulets that flopped massively against the bulges in the blouse). Along the outer seams of the blouse and down the front of it were the mere remnants of what must have once been machine embroidery, in what must have once been bright, dazzling colors; they were now faded tatters sticking grimly to the fabric of the garment.

Madame Zoruba's head was covered down to her forehead with a rag that made no attempt to disguise itself. It was filthy and disreputable and tight against her skull, held with a giant safety pin. Bits of frazzled hair protruded from all the edges of the scarf, kinky from the chemicals of home permanents and home blackening procedures.

Her face was brown with age, and round, with great empty sacs of skin under the eyes and along the mouth. The eyes, however, gave life to the woman. The eyes seemed somehow capable of listening, apart and for themselves. Her mouth, which worked constantly, was a brownish pit in her face and the few teeth that remained were blackened stumps, uneven and deformed, noisily clicking against each other in irregular pairs. I wondered, in some despair, at the feelings of those girls and women who had come here, to this woman, to find solutions to their overwhelming problems.

Charlie's voice was hushed with concern, and now and then I could catch a few of the Polish phrases, vaguely similar to the Slovak language of my husband's parents. The girl . . . very young . . . the girl, again. Each time he would turn his face toward me. Madame Zoruba watched us both, her eyes moving swiftly, flashing first at me, then at Charlie, sizing us up, taking our measure.

When she spoke, the words of her language were indistinguishable: a mere series of wet, slippery, sputtering and guttural sounds, rapidly spit out with much gesturing of the shoulders and clinking of the beads and teeth. Suddenly and without warning, at least without warning that I could comprehend, she whirled toward me with a flourish of skirts and planted her face inches from mine, looking into my eyes, her own eyes flickering back and forth, studying whatever she saw there. Then she nodded brusquely, backed away. She motioned me to another chair, switched on a yellow lamp and sat on the footstool, her knees wide apart, skirts reaching to the floor. She motioned for my hand, pushed back my left and grasped my right hand. She covered my hand with both of hers and rubbed it roughly; her palms were like chips of rock and they grated. Then she rested my hand lightly in her own and squinted and frowned at my palm, tracing lines from beginnings to endings with a stubby yellow fingernail. She hunched over and made a hawking sound in her throat, and I was almost convinced that she was about to spit into my hand, but she merely made some growling, gagging sounds in her throat. She studied my hand so intently, and with such mutterings and squintings and concern that I began to feel there *was* something written there, unreadable to me, but known to her. Her concentration seemed complete, and she dug her stumpy nail deeper and deeper into my palm, then twisted my hand over, rubbed the back with a horny palm, and turned it palm upward again. Then, she placed her face into my hand, and her breath felt hot and moist and dirty and I could feel it along my arm and down my neck and between my shoulders, but I sat rigid and unmoving.

Finally, she tossed my hand back to me: she had seen all she had to see. It was all there.

For the first time, she spoke to me and her English was as guttural and nearly as incomprehensible as her Polish had been. "You are two months with this thing?"

It was not really a question but a declaration, and I nodded. It was a good measure of her shrewdness: two months was just about right. The first month, the man would tell the woman that maybe she's just late, maybe she's just upset. But when the second month had passed, she knew for sure, and if something was to be done, this was the time to do it, when she entered the third month.

She ignored me then, not even favoring me with her

sly squinty glances, but spoke to Charlie, who stood awkwardly, his hat held in both hands, shifting from one foot to the other. They spoke in low tones, excluding me, and she turned and waddled from the room, trailing beads from the doorway behind her. I glanced over at Charlie, but he was studying his feet, and then Madame Zoruba was back with her hand extended toward me. She opened her hand and showed a small piece of pink tissue paper in which rested two white pills. She bent her face low over them, muttered, wetly spattering the tablets, then took my hand, pressed the little package into it, breathed on it a few times, her lips moving wetly, then closed my hand into a fist.

"Tonight," she said, "at nine o'clock. Take. Maybe no more trouble." Then, shrugging her shoulders, "Maybe no good. Who knows?"

Charlie spoke again to the woman, and she shrugged and shook her head, offering him no assurances, then gestured for us to follow her into the second room, through the beaded doorway.

The room was painted some dark color, and heavy black or navy blue drapes of a lush material, possibly velvet, hung over the window. There was scuffed linoleum on the floor, but it was so dark in the room it was impossible to guess its color. Against one wall was a kind of altar, a hodgepodge collection of semireligious items. There was a crucifix with a dreadful looking Jesus, all chipped plaster, and painted blood oozing down his wrists and forehead. Artificial flowers—fuchsia and brilliant yellows and oranges—the kind some people buy to put on graves on Memorial Day, were ranged along the altar, and the altar cloth was decorated with grotesque embroidered figures and designs. A cloth behind the crucifix was decked out with stars and half-moons and strange symbols. There was a brass bell resting on the altar, and several jars of incense candles, all unlit. In the center of the altar was a large brass box with a huge padlock and a wide slit in the center, and a little card hung from the padlock, apparently written with some Polish words of solicitation.

It was a stifling, cramped room; the air was dusty and dry and stale. Madame Zoruba handed each of us a long taper and then lit them from a book of matches. Then she indicated the incense candles, and as we lit them, she made a strange cry.

She stood behind me, her hands raised over my head, her face turned up to the ceiling, wailing thickly and heavily. Charlie watched her, his face unreadable in the flickering candlelight. Then, her incantation over, she spoke to him, indicating her cash box, and he pulled out a five-dollar bill from his wallet. She caught his hand mid-air and spoke rapidly, her eyes narrowing. Charlie then dug back into his wallet and came up with a twenty-dollar bill, which she examined, slobbered over and placed into her brass box with a few muttered words. Then she harshly blew out the candles, but not soon enough, for the sickeningly sweet perfume had already penetrated our clothing and hair and skin. We walked back into the first room, and Madame Zoruba took my arm roughly.

"Take pills," she said. "Wait two days. Nothing happen—you come see me again."

I nodded and started after Charlie for the door leading to the street, when she suddenly caught my arm again, turning me toward her. Looking fully into my face, her eyes bright and cruel, she said, "This one—here," poking into my stomach, "no good, see?" She circled her face with her hand, then jabbed her index finger and her thumb into her eyes. "No good, see? No eyes, this one. What is word, hah? Blind. This one here," again poking my stomach, *"blind.* No good. Not have the eyes!"

We walked down the street silently, staring straight ahead. I felt lightheaded from the smell and atmosphere of the place, from the clinging, trailing incense. We walked slowly, heavily, each of us caught up in it. Driving back to B.O.S.S., I noticed that Charlie's face was gray, drawn, his mouth pulled down slightly at the corners.

The pills were aspirin. Madame Zoruba could not be arrested for dispensing medicine without a license. Anyone can give you an aspirin.

The money she had demanded from Charlie was a

donation for her religious order. And Madame Zoruba could not be arrested for predicting the future for a fee.

Two days later, we appeared again at Madame Zoruba's. Reentering these premises was enough to make me feel ill, and apparently my appearance satisfied her, for she studied me carefully, nodding now and again, then stood back from me, speaking to Charlie about me as though I were some statue or object in the room. Charlie spoke with his head down, his toe scuffing, his hands twitching and spinning the hat he held, shaking his head. Madame Zoruba made clicking, swallowing noises, speaking something to Charlie, jutting her round chin at me, waving her hands in front of her face, pounding her stomach a few times. Then she motioned for me to sit. She waddled away for a moment and returned holding a piece of paper and a pencil, which she thrust at me. Then she eyed Charlie, motioned him to the next room, stood watching the swaying beads until they became still.

"Write this," she whispered at me. "Yah, now write this. 426 West 87th Street. 16-A. Two days from now." Shaking her head for a moment, in some confusion, counting on her fingers. "Two days: today Tuesday. Wednesday. *Thursday*. Write down, write down."

I wrote it down.

"Seven-thirty. Nighttime. Write down."

She watched the words forming on the paper, then shook my arm and held up five fingers, stretched apart. "Five hundred, you bring. He say . . . that man, he say okay." I nodded.

Then she stood away from me and motioned me into her inner sanctum again, where Charlie stood waiting. We went through the whole routine again, and Charlie parted with another twenty-dollar bill, and we were covered again by the heavy fragrance.

Just before we left, she crept up close to me and squinted her eyes tightly shut, losing them in a network of crumpled wrinkles and motioned with her hand wildly. "That one," she said, "no good. Blind, blind, no eyes, no see."

And then we left Madame Zoruba's with the address of

the abortionist in my pocketbook—in my handwriting and unwitnessed.

The building was a rooming house occupied by those faceless world-weary transients who appear one day with enough money for a week's rent, blend into the bleakness of the surroundings and then move on without ever having existed within the walls of their featureless rooms. As soon as we left Madame Zoruba's, Charlie made a few phone calls, then told me very briefly what had taken place. He had had the premises checked out and found that 16-A was on a long-lease basis, occupied only occasionally by a "Mr. Dormanski." Mr. Dormanski was not at home at the moment, and a few dollars and a concocted story to the janitor of the building would give our men time to "prepare things."

"Prepare things," I knew, meant they were going to bug the rooms. Charlie didn't say too much, because as in all such matters, the fewer persons who know the details, the better. All I did know was that the rooms would be bugged by the time I arrived for my appointment, and that other police officers would be at listening posts somewhere in the building and would take appropriate action at the appropriate time. That was all I needed to know, and that was all Charlie told me.

I couldn't sleep much Wednesday night, as the events of the next night were working over and over in my mind. I had an appointment for seven-thirty the next night to have an abortion. My tossing and pacing of course kept Tony from sleeping, which was probably what I had in mind, because he finally got up and made me a cup of tea. This is the standard thing my husband does for me when I am tired, irritable, excited, nasty, sweet, happy, unhappy, quarrelsome. I have lived half my life inside a cup of bitter, unsugared tea with just a drop of milk. He never asks if I want a cup of tea—I never even know he's boiling it up. He just hands it to me and I drink it and then usually say what it is I have to say. If there has been one symbolic thing in our marriage, one thing that represents love and devotion and understanding, that one thing would be a cup of tea.

I thought about the assignment all the next day as I was poking around our little apartment, watching the clock. In so many hours, I will have left here, covered my assignment and be back here and it will all be over. Tony called at noon, and I told him I was fine and that I would leave his dinner in the refrigerator. All he had to do was heat it up; the meat was all cooked. He said okay, that he'd see me when I got home. If he was asleep, no matter what time it was, I was to wake him.

Charlie called me at five-thirty and told me everything was set up and I wasn't to worry about a thing. He and three other squad men were set up in a room on the third floor. Apartment 16-A was on the first floor, rear; there was one small room in the front and a larger one in back. They had bugged both rooms, and they would break in the minute they had what they wanted. He told me to show up about five minutes before my appointment, and he told me everything would be fine. Charlie's voice had the calm, certain assurance of the professional policeman, and I carried the knowledge with me that he would be near by.

I always shiver and sweat at the same time. My teeth chatter and I have to clench them together, because if I take a breath through my mouth, they bang together like a child's on a winter day. It wasn't particularly cold; it was the end of March and there was already a trace of spring in the night air. The front door of the building was open, and I pushed my way in to the typical, narrow, dark hallway. There was one uncovered yellow bulb which streaked the narrow passageway, showing all the bulges and lumps of plaster which were held on the wall by a covering of shiny brown paint. The linoleum on the floor was fairly clean, but pieces had broken off and a bug scampered out of a large hole in the center of the floor. I pulled my arms close against my sides: you never let your clothing touch these walls, and you have to watch for cockroaches dropping from the ceiling. Apartment 16-A was located directly behind the tall, high stairway, and the number was nearly rubbed off the door

There was no bell, so I knocked. Maybe no one would answer.

The door opened instantly and a woman looked out. "Yes?"

"I . . . I was supposed to come here."

"Yes?" she asked again.

"Yes. I . . . Madame Zoruba said at seven-thirty."

The woman opened the door, standing in the doorway so that I had to enter almost sideways to avoid her, and then she closed the door behind her. I heard a series of locks or bolts or something, sealing us in.

"Stay here," she said, then left for the other room. When she opened the door, I could see a brightness, the glimpse of a man's arm, heard muttering voices. The room was very small with no window, and I stood dead center, not wanting to sit on the sagging heavy couch. A few minutes went by, and I sat down on the edge of a wooden chair, taking in none of the details of the room, straining to hear the conversation in the next room. It was apparently in a foreign language, for it sounded like a humming, formless murmuring: two men, one woman. I looked around the room, vaguely wondering where the microphone was planted. I leaped to my feet when the woman flung open the door.

She had a card in her hand and she went to the small table against one wall and motioned me toward her, indicating that I should pull over a chair. She switched on a small light which was set into the wall. It was fluorescent, and the purplish-blue light made her short-cropped bleached hair almost green. She was a short, solid woman with small, hard, grubby hands and a dirty, flowered house dress. Her feet, which she kept tapping flatly on the floor, were encased in cracked white gum-soled shoes, and there were lumps near the small toes.

"So," she said. "I am Mrs. Poland. You will answer these questions. Are you married?"

"No," I said loudly. She looked up sharply and then I remembered that the microphones were supersensitive. I fumbled with my fingers nervously as she marked something on the card.

"When was your last period?"

"Beginning of January."

"You are in good health?" She turned to study me and her face was the face of every rotten, unfeeling teacher who had ever gotten into the profession by mistake—a face that could look at a weeping schoolgirl and say, "Your tears don't move *me,* young lady, they don't impress *me,*" because she had never had any tears of her own. Her eyes were small pebbles of meanness, blunted with uneven lashes and framed by unplucked brows set too low. It was a cruelly disinterested face, and she looked at me without seeing me. We went through a series of questions: height, 5′ 5″; weight, 115 pounds; no heart trouble; no high or low blood pressure; not given to fainting spells.

"And you do not carry on, right?" she asked in a hoarse whisper. "You do not make a fuss about things, eh?"

"What do you mean?"

"You ever have cramps with your periods?"

"Sometimes."

"Good," she said, "then you will know what it will feel like. You will have some cramps, a few bad ones maybe. I will give you something so it will not be so bad, but I will tell you this now, and you will remember it."

There was a coldness in her voice as she leaned forward, pointing the ballpoint pen at me. There was a menacing set to her mouth and her small eyes. "There will be no sound in that room, no sound." She pointed to the back room as though it were an execution chamber. "The doctors are good men and know what they are doing, but they will stand for no nonsense. They must have silence, and if you cry out or make a noise," she held the pen straight in the air, "one single noise, they will be very angry and it will not go well for you. You understand this?"

I nodded. The sweat was pouring down the sides of my body, clammy and cold. "Yes."

"Then you will give me the money."

I dug into my pocketbook, which contained no gun or shield or identification in my own name, and took the five one-hundred-dollar bills from my wallet. They were treated with a chemical that would coat the hands with an invisible phosphorescent substance which would show up under a special lamp, and the serial numbers had been recorded. As soon as I handed her the money, a man burst from the other room and came to her side, watching her count the five bills. She turned to him with a look of pure hatred.

"Five," she said angrily. "What did you think—I cheat you?" She shoved the money to him, and he left the room with a whisper of words. He hadn't even glanced at me.

"Now," Mrs. Poland said, "one other thing. Afterward, you will stay here for one hour. You will drink the coffee I give you and . . ."

For some incomprehensible reason, I said, "I can't drink coffee—it makes me sick. Could I have tea?"

She narrowed her eyes at me. "Coffee is a great stimulant—you will drink it as a medicine, and then you will leave here. You will walk out of here alone and without any sound, and you will walk slowly to the corner. There are many taxicabs on the corner and you will go wherever you wish. And now," she lowered her voice and leaned forward, her face close to mine, "you will never come back here or look for us again. We will not be here. And you will tell no one or you will be in terrible trouble. Do you believe that?"

"Yes."

"Wait here." She left the room again and returned immediately with a hypodermic needle in her hand, holding it up to the light. Some shiny yellowish fluid ran down, then up the length of it as she approached me.

"Roll up your sleeve," she said, taking my right arm. I froze from my neck down, unable to move, not wanting whatever was in the needle, but she grabbed my arm and pushed the sleeve of my sweater up and injected the stuff into my veins.

"What was it?" I asked. "What was the injection?" (Oh, Charlie, hear it. They injected me with something.)

"It will relax you. You ask too many questions. Come." The back room was brightly lit, and the two men had put on short white coats and were busy at a long table. In the center of the room was a kind of table with a thin, hard mattress.

Mrs. Poland handed me a white dressing gown. "Take off your clothes and put this on with the opening in the back and lie on the table."

I saw a dirty pail, a wash pail on the floor next to the table, and my foot kicked it, or the pail seemed to kick my foot. The drug was taking hold, enveloping me in a kind of sleepy nausea. "What is the pail for?" I asked, the words thick and slow.

Mrs. Poland said, "What do you think the pail is for? Come now, get undressed."

I stood leaning against the table staring at the pail, and I was aware that I was crying, because I could feel the sobs and feel the tears. But I didn't remember starting to cry, and I could hear Mrs. Poland talking to the two men, the doctors, busy with their preparations. The pail is for the baby, I said, the pail is for my baby, for I was going to have this abortion and no one was going to help me, no one was going to stop it, it was going to happen. She said my child had no eyes; she said my child was blind.

One of them, one of those "doctors" stood in front of me and looked down at my eyes, not speaking to me, not saying one word to me, just looking at my eyes. I could see his face enlarged in terrible detail: black, thick brows meeting over the bridge of his nose and bearing down on his black eyes. His nose and cheeks were covered with small black pits, and his face was blurred and smeared. I pressed my hands against my stomach and leaned against the table crying and crying, not seeing Charlie or the others who were suddenly in the room. I heard, or rather sensed, the confusion, the rushing about, the moving of bodies, the doctors against the wall, Mrs. Poland cursing and shrieking, spitting bitter words at me and at the other two men, blaming them, blaming me. I leaned against Charlie's shoulder sickly, and he was smiling and saying something to me. All I could think of was that my child could not be blind and could not end up in that filthy pail on the floor.

No one had known that I was pregnant. It was really not possible to know for sure, except that *I knew*. I told Tony that night, when it was over. Even though I was only ten days late, I knew that I was pregnant; I had known, I told him, at the moment of conception, had known all the time while Madame Zoruba had looked at my hand and muttered and told me that my child would be blind; I knew I had a child growing, forming, and she had said those terrible things. I drank tea and told him the full horror of it now. I had truly been some girl alone with those people and that pail on the floor.

One of the two men was an illegal immigrant who had entered the country via Mexico. He had come from Europe to Canada to Cuba to the Pan American countries, to Mexico, to the United States, to New York, to West 87th Street, to apartment 16-A. The other was a doctor who had lost his license years earlier for abortion and suspected illegal dispensation of narcotics. Mrs. Poland had been a practical nurse, had run a rooming house, had sold shoes in a store that specialized in custom-built footgear for peculiar foot problems. The men and Mrs. Poland were indicted for attempted abortion, found guilty and sentenced to a year each. The illegal immigrant had his sentence suspended and was turned over to the United States Department of Immigration.

Madame Zoruba went free: we had no case against her strong enough to stand up. Madame Zoruba is probably telling her fortunes still, making her dread predictions and whispering an address, a time and location to frantic girls and abandoned women.

I took a leave of absence from the Police Department in July, and our daughter was born in November. When she was put into my arms, her eyes were large and blue and the crinkles under them indicated that they would be even larger and wider—to encompass the world around her, to see and to look and to find and to question. Holding her, Tracy, with Tony's face in delicate miniature, I felt a terrible pity and sorrow for all women, for all girls who have entered apartment 16-A and all the rooms like it, alone, to leave their futures and their dreams and their hopes in some dirty pail on the floor.

11

"The jagged eye of justice"

When my daughter was nearly six months old, I returned to the Department and spent two weeks at the Women's Bureau before being assigned to the Pickpocket Squad. It was spring, and it was a relief to get out of the office and into the sweet air of the park again. My partner was an amiable, slow-moving man who took his time and seemed to realize I was having some slight difficulties in getting back into it. I missed moves, my reflexes had slowed. What had once been natural had to be learned over again now: the quick encompassing glance at a crowd, the sharp, easily defined points of concentration.

"Relax," my partner said, "it's just like swimming. You can stay away from it for twenty years, but let somebody throw you in the river and you'll tread around a while, getting the feel of it, and next thing you know, you'll be swimming just as good as ever."

On our fourth tour, we connected. We spotted him simultaneously: the one "wrong" element in a crowd. He was invisible or nonexistent to the other people visiting the zoo, but marked for us by that almost indefinable "something about him." He was a young Puerto Rican pickpocket and we nabbed him on a grand larceny charge. Since he was unable to put up bail, his trial came up within the week. It was the first time I had ever taken part in a jury trial, and it was the first time I ever saw Judge Melvin Goldhaber. I had heard of him, of course.

Judge Melvin Goldhaber was a majestic-looking man in his early fifties with a smooth pink face and thick sparkling white hair worn long, tapering regally behind his ears. It was rumored that he trimmed it himself.

Vanity shone from his light blue eyes and was evident in the tilt of his chin, set just a trifle too high, so that the spectators had full benefit of his nearly perfect profile. He had long, slender fingers, like a musician, and whether he used them to tap a pencil, pound a desk or stab the air to reinforce a point, his gestures were calculated and spellbinding. The illusion of physical beauty was shattered, however, the moment he spoke, for the growling rough voice testified to a Lower East Side boyhood; none of the refining elements of higher education had tempered this ugly sound. Hearing the voice (and closing your eyes), you pictured the speaker as short and dumpy and muscular with black stubble on chin and cheek. The shock was reinforced because the graceful gestures of the hands were at odds with the delivery of the words. He had a strangely "unfinished" quality, yet he seemed to relish his impact on those around him.

Judge Goldhaber had served what must have seemed to him endless years as a magistrate in the lower courts. Perhaps to break the boredom he had started to liven up the week-end night sessions. He had sensed an alert and appreciative reaction from the young college students out on a cheap date, and he began to make low jokes at and around the various derelicts brought before him. Eventually, he was considered "the thing to do" on a dull Friday or Saturday night. Playing more and more to his audience, Magistrate Goldhaber administered his version of justice on the basis of what seemed good for the "house." He began inserting amusingly bitter little speeches and asides (holding his hand up to the court stenographer whenever necessary), and everyone seemed to appreciate his efforts—everyone, that is, except the culprit, who usually was some befuddled drunk, not too sure what his particular role in all this proceeding was supposed to be. There was scarcely a policeman in New York City who couldn't regale a group of his fellow officers with a good "Goldie" story.

When, through the machinations of the political machine, his various efforts, good press and patience were rewarded with a judgeship in General Sessions, "Goldie" found himself enthroned in a vaster theater. The fact that the attorneys trying the various cases saw no humor in his not-too-subtle direction of a case had no other effect on him than that his elegant hand would wave away all protests, valid or otherwise. During his five years as a judge he was cited some seven or eight times by various lawyers to various committees for various forms of unbecoming conduct, but this bothered him not at all. He had taken measure of these lawyers. He knew them well, and considered them not much better than the garbage they represented. He knew which ones were the trouble-makers, which ones were constantly trying to nail him down (no one had succeeded: just let them try!).

Judge Goldhaber had a real sense of the times, a feeling for the people. He characterized the riffraff appearing before him as "rat-punks." In *his* court it was *his* show, and his responsibility was to the people of what he liked to call "our fair city." He knew he was right, for he had a collection of clippings—editorials from the largest daily newspaper in New York City citing him for his efforts toward stiffer sentences and quicker justice. He appeared on various radio shows with calm placidity and self-assurance, unbothered by his own gutter tones in denouncing the lice and vermin that were ruining our fair city— sounding for all the world like some escaped convict, yet leaning heavily on his physical appearance.

Judge Goldhaber had the righteous citizen's outrage toward the punk-hoodlums who put the "people of this city" to the expense of a trial, when obviously they were all guilty. His sworn enemy—as the people's representative and as the tool of justice—was any bastard who stood before him accused of a first-degree crime who refused to accept a lesser plea, refused his good offer to "cop out." Goldie would lower his sculptured chin and draw his silvered brows together and flick his elegant finger at the protesting thug. Then you'll stand trial, he'd growl, and in *my court,* and you will get the maximum: this was his always fulfilled promise. It was a wise attorney who talked a client into "copping out" in Goldie's court.

But Minnie Drexel was not a wise attorney in the eyes

of her colleagues, and she was a fool in the eyes of Judge Goldhaber. Her non-paying, Legal Aid clients, with only time to lose, hoping always for the miracle—which was nowhere evident in Judge Goldhaber's domain—occasionally stuck with their not-guilty pleas.

We all knew Mrs. Drexel: poor old Minnie. Whether people were discussing how she won a case, made a point, blasted the cop or cried openly in court over the defendant, or whether they were admiring her grudgingly for her relentless loyalty to her clients or ridiculing her emotionalism in losing a case, they always called her "poor old Minnie." Not that she was so old; it seemed to me more that she was ageless, with a driving kind of energy and a quickness and sharpness not expected from the somewhat dumpy, matronly figure. Her voice had a carrying quality but was devoid of the fullness and resonance of her male colleagues in the Legal Aid battery. Her sound carried the way a scolding mother's voice carries: nagging, repeating the same phrases incessantly until she was satisfied with the response or until an exasperated district attorney objected to a glassy-eyed judge that the witness *had* answered the question. Then poor old Minnie would spin around, glaring at the district attorney, and call out: "But not to my satisfaction! Not to *my* satisfaction!"

Every police officer was suspect in her eyes; we were filled with treachery which she must unravel bit by bit. Layer by layer, she would try to explore the hidden motivations inherent in the act of accusing an itinerant laborer of theft, an illiterate girl of prostitution, a nineteen-year-old immigrant of rape. Her method of defense was furious accusation; every police officer knew it and was wary of Minnie. Poor old Minnie and her bevy of losers.

I had never faced Mrs. Drexel on a witness stand, but I had often seen this small, shrill dynamo in action, had seen the beet-faced policeman fall helplessly into her traps while the other officers in court moaned inwardly as one of their brothers went sprawling feet-first or headlong into unguarded statements or remarks which poor old Minnie pounced on with triumph and cutting scorn.

In my direct testimony I described the details of the arrest: my partner and I had observed the defendant removing a wallet from the back pocket of an unsuspecting father of two little boys who were watching the seals at the Central Park Zoo. I answered the brisk questions of the district attorney, who nodded, waving a hand at Mrs. Drexel. I leaned back slightly in the witness chair, taking a long deep breath, letting my eyes scan the room. There was a high white slash of dusty sunlight streaking across the center of the courtroom, and the indistinguishable figures sitting along the polished oak rows were like lifeless statues spotlighted in a department store window. Several attorneys were seated in the front row, just back of the rail that enclosed the various tables and chairs and benches reserved for the attorneys trying cases, the defendant, witnesses, police officers and complainants. The jury was a blur of faces to my left. The district attorney, a man with thick sandy hair and the build of a slightly undersized football player, tilted back in his chair, speaking with some expensively dressed woman who leaned over the railing with the elegance of a bored young society matron.

"You're Detective Uhnak? Hmm, yes. Miss or Mrs. Uhnak?"

"Mrs.," I answered.

Mrs. Drexel seemed distracted by a clutch of papers in her hands and did not raise her face. "Yes then, Mrs. Uhnak. And how long have you been a police officer?"

"Nearly three years."

"And how long have you been a detective?" She still kept her face down.

"About a year."

"And you're a good police officer?" Mrs. Drexel asked, raising her face to mine.

"Yes. I think so. I try to be."

Mrs. Drexel's voice was impatient, and she fluttered the papers in front of her. "Oh yes, you're a good police officer—I've seen you in court, day after day, testifying. Down in Special Sessions. I've seen you."

The remark was an accusation: I've seen you. I stiffened, watching the woman's face—a flexible, mobile face, twitching with words. Mrs. Drexel had started her cross-examination at the angry pitch usually built up slowly by the male attorneys after the smooth, syrupy politeness of identification. But Mrs. Drexel had no time for slow-building irritations, and she began with an anger that often led her directly into a full-blown fury.

"Now, let me see. You observed this boy," turning to the defendant, fluttering her papers in his direction, "first at three o'clock last June 7 by the seal pond in the Central Park Zoo?"

"No," I said. "The time of the arrest was three o'clock. I first observed him at 2:20 P.M. by the lion cage."

Mrs. Drexel frowned, squinted, her face puzzled. "By the lion cage? We haven't heard about the lion cage before. What was he doing by the lion cage?"

I answered softly, "Watching the lion."

There was a small sound of amusement in the courtroom and Mrs. Drexel whirled about, leaning her head downward to peer over the tops of her glasses; then she spun back to me. "And that struck you as unusual, and so you watched him, because he was observing the lion?"

"No. I observed him first at the lion cage, and then he began moving. He moved toward the . . ."

Mrs. Drexel held up both her hands, and a paper fell from her grasp to her feet, unnoticed. "Wait a minute, wait a minute. You noticed him at the lion cage. Whom else did you notice at the lion cage?"

"There were other people there."

"Describe them! What did they look like? Who were these 'other people'? What were they doing?"

I shook my head, shrugged; I couldn't see her point. "Other people. I didn't notice them particularly, because they did nothing to arouse my suspicions."

"But the defendant aroused your suspicions, just standing there, looking at the lion?"

"When he began moving, he aroused my suspicions."

"No, no, wait. We will go back, I want to know *exactly,*" Mrs. Drexel said, stressing the word, as though it were the key to a perplexing and important secret, *"exactly* why you noticed him standing there watching the lion, in a great crowd of people who were doing exactly the same thing. Why *him?*"

"There wasn't a great crowd," I said steadily, "there were maybe four, five people, some children. And the defendant."

"Yes, yes, go on," Mrs. Drexel said, blinking impatiently.

I took a deep, slow breath. "And then, the defendant began moving . . ."

Mrs. Drexel stamped her foot. "No! No, don't get him moving. I want to know . . ."

The district attorney held up his hand at me, pulling his lips between his fingers as he rose. "Your Honor, I think Mrs. Drexel will have us at the lion cage all day. Will she concede that the officer saw the defendant at the lion cage and that the defendant then moved on?"

Mrs. Drexel's voice crackled loudly. "I won't concede anything! I want to know why this police officer picked out this boy among all those other people just standing there watching the lion. That is her testimony, those are her words. Why this caused her to be suspicious of him. That's what I want to know!"

The judge made a deep rumbling sound, ignoring Mrs. Drexel's angry glare. He spread out his palms toward the jury and shrugged slightly, helplessly, and the jury made appreciative soft sounds. When the woman began to speak again, he held his hands up toward her, and leaned toward the witness chair, and said, softly, rationally, in contrast to Mrs. Drexel's tones: "Officer, why did you notice the defendant and not the other folks watching the lion?"

I answered the judge, not looking at Mrs. Drexel, but feeling her eyes on my face. "He called attention to himself by his manner. He was jumpy, nervous, edgy. He just didn't 'look right.' "

The judge flicked his hand at Mrs. Drexel, smiled and

leaned back in his chair, but Mrs. Drexel leaped at my last words. *"He just didn't look right,* eh? You didn't like his looks?" She didn't stop for an answer, but continued a barrage of angry questions. "He looked dirty? Something like that? Out of place? Were there any other *Puerto Ricans* in the crowd watching the lion? Or was he the only one?"

That was what she had been building to. I clamped down on my teeth, then answered slowly, in a tightly controlled voice, "Which question do you want me to answer, Mrs. Drexel? I've lost track."

She jutted out her jaw: don't get smart with me. "Just this one, then. Was he the only *Puerto Rican* there?"

The judge slapped his hand on the top of his desk flatly. "Come on, come on, Mrs. Drexel, none of that stuff," he said roughly.

"I want to know. It's pertinent. I feel it's pertinent."

I didn't look for any signals. I answered quickly, coldly, "I couldn't say, Mrs. Drexel."

"Well, *he's* Puerto Rican, isn't he? Could you say that much?"

"Yes."

"Anyone could see that, even if he were in a crowd, right?"

The judge spoke loudly, suddenly, so that the sound of his voice made me jump. He pointed brusquely at the defendant and the jury's eyes followed his outstretched hand. "Anyone can see he's a Puerto Rican. Okay, Mrs. Drexel?" And then he called across the space separating him from the defendant, "Are you a Puerto Rican, mister? Huh? Speak English, mister?"

The defendant, a sallow, thin boy of twenty-three, suddenly aware of the attention focused on him and no understanding it, grinned foolishly and lifted his hand in a confused half-salute to the judge and nodded his head up and down in a kind of greeting.

"Yeah, he's a Puerto Rican. He just said so. Okay, Mrs. Drexel?"

The woman's face flushed down to her neck and she smashed the sheaf of papers against the side of her thigh

Judge Goldhaber, I object," she shouted, "I object to these tactics and I intend . . ."

The judge's voice was full and rich now, filling the courtroom. "And *I* object to these tactics of yours. Get on with it. Make all your objections later, in written form, like you usually do. Get on with it, get on with it."

Mrs. Drexel stood motionless, frozen, her eyes on the judge. Watching her face, I felt a great, lunging sensation in my chest and stomach, and was unable to glance at the judge or the jury or at the spectators in the room. I felt my own face redden, felt some strange, unknown humiliation. But Mrs. Drexel turned to me slowly, and her face was completely composed, the color normal.

"All right, then," she said calmly. "After you became suspicious of him because he was standing there, watching the lion, *then* what did you observe?"

"Hold it," the judge called out noisily, addressing the jury now. "The officer was suspicious of him because of his nervous, jumpy, edgy manner." And then he turned to me, smiling. "Isn't that right, officer? Isn't that what you said?"

I did not want this ally, did not want to be a partner to this man. Seeing nothing, just the haze of the room, I answered, "Yes, sir."

"Good. Yes. Continue," he said, waving at Mrs. Drexel.

Mrs. Drexel continued as though there had been no interruption. "What did you observe then?"

"The defendant walked over to the monkey cages and . . ."

The sharp voice broke into my words. "Were there other people watching the monkeys?"

I had a strange sensation of being far away from my questioner, as though the demands were coming from some far, hollow place, and my responses sounded empty. "Yes, and then he . . ."

"What other people?" Mrs. Drexel demanded. "What did they look like? Who were they?"

Mrs. Drexel asked her questions totally oblivious to the soft, expectant moan in the courtroom. I watched her curiously, wondering how the woman could deliberately

expose herself to the waiting judge. Everyone else in th
room held his breath; all eyes now turned to the bench.

I did not answer. My silence was almost an anticipate
pause, as though we were all in some play; the judg
had the next lines. He sat silently, majestically buildin
his anger around him, until all eyes were on him. Onl
Mrs. Drexel, seemingly totally unaware, awaited my ar
swer.

"Oh, no," the judge said, in a whining, groaning voic
and only then did Mrs. Drexel look at him. "Oh, no. We'r
not playing that game again. We've been through th
whole bit, and you are not going to play tricks with th
court!"

Mrs. Drexel stared at him in honest amazement. "
am trying to elicit some *facts* here, your Honor. I war
to know some *things* here," she said, now pointing at m
"I want to know just what's so terrible about a youn
Puerto Rican kid watching some lions and monkeys at th
zoo, why our police officers think it's a suspicious thin
That's what I want to know."

I heard the sounds of the argument, the shrill, high
demanding voice and the heavy, powerful voice of author
ity, but not the words, because the meaning of Mrs. Drex
el's method was building inside of me. The woman wa
attempting to twist me into a mold, a pattern of her ow
making, and I felt a wave of resentment toward the wom
an, far removed from the long-time sniping contempt o
the judge and the contemptuous amusement of the jur
Openly, without reason or justification of any kind, Mr
Drexel was making me out as a bigot. I glanced at th
jury and then at the defendant, sitting at the long, shinin
table, rubbing the palms of his hands absently on th
silky-smooth surface. He seemed faded, grayed by h
confinement; his eyes seemed stale, with no trace of th
black sparkle. His clothing, probably provided by son
relative, was crumpled and too big for him and his skinn
neck stood away from the yellowing white collar whic
was pulled together by a wide, brightly designed blue an
green tie. He was twenty-three but he had the face of a
old child; a resigned child, for he smiled quickly wheneve

Mrs. Drexel glanced at him or a court attendant poked him. Then his face would lapse into a staring, uncomprehending blankness. This courtroom was just a place to him, as his prison cell was just a place to him.

I looked at the jury of his peers—for that was what he was supposed to be entitled to. A large woman, fanning her perspiring face with her ringed hand, leaned heavily against her chair, crowding a middle-aged, well-groomed woman who probably smelled of some tangy, fruit-flavored toilet water. She looked like a woman who was aware of doing her share, of fulfilling her part of public responsibility. A white-haired man occupied the foreman's chair, and his fire-red, vein-scarred face and swollen nose were in startling contrast to the whiteness of his hair, which was lank and fell against the sparkling silver frame of his eyeglasses. He carefully pushed it back from time to time with long, clean fingers. He was studying the defendant; his mouth was cast downward, and he whispered something to the man next to him. They both stared at Paco Hernández, who stared into space.

The rest of the jury seemed intent on the judge's words, aware of the uniqueness of their position, aware that the famous man was playing to them. Appreciative of the honor, they gave their reactions quickly: the stifled, court-acceptable laugh, the stiff, discerning, disapproving silences. The district attorney was glancing at his wrist watch, looking at the streak of sunlight from the window up near the ceiling. Judge Goldhaber was fighting his battle for him. I felt no alliance with anyone in the room; I felt removed from the wrangling which actually was revolving around me.

Finally, the shrill voice was silenced, and the judge's voice rumbled to a halt. Then Mrs. Drexel approached me, looking unruffled, fresh, ready. "All right, then, we're at the monkey cages. What did you observe the defendant do next?"

I blinked rapidly, bringing my mind into focus, trying to alert myself to the moment. "Yes, the defendant watched the monkeys for a moment or two, and then began to move among the people standing near him."

"That was suspicious? That he moved a bit?"

"To me it was," I answered stiffly. "I knew what he was looking for."

Mrs. Drexel regarded me silently for a moment, her face hard and still. Then her voice rasped out in the angry tone of the school-teacher to the class cheat, "You knew that he was looking around at the people, but don't tell me what thoughts were inside this boy's head!"

I felt the resentment; I wanted to be free of this woman's voice and stares and nasty, digging words. But knowing that the anger, released, would be dangerous, would interfere with my words, I spoke carefully, consciously and with great effort, keeping my voice from trembling or betraying me in any way. "He was looking around in a manner that I considered suspicious. I then observed him walk over to the seal pool." And then, for no reason that I could fathom, or perhaps without a reason, perhaps just by a natural falling-in with the pattern established in the room, I said quietly, rhythmically, "And I don't know how many people were standing there, or what they looked like, or who they were, or if any of them happened to be *Puerto Ricans!*"

There was a loud burst of laughter from the judge, echoed by sounds throughout the courtroom. "Good, officer," he said, between gasps, "you've saved us some considerable debate, I would say."

I felt an immediate regret, a hot flushing shame, and there was a look of pure and open hatred and disgust on Mrs. Drexel's face. "Go on, officer, what did you observe then?"

"I observed the defendant move in back of an unidentified woman and place his hand on the clasp of her pocketbook. He then moved away and . . ."

"Wait a minute, wait a minute." Again, the quick insistent voice, delving into some deep, hidden pi wherein might lie the truth of the matter. "You observed him put his hand on a woman's pocketbook? Wha woman?"

"An unidentified woman."

Mrs. Drexel rubbed her chin fiercely. "You observe

him place his hand on a woman's pocketbook? You're a police officer? What action did you take at this point?"

"I continued my observation and then . . ."

"No, no, no!" Mrs. Drexel was shaking her head and waving her hands filled with papers of various sizes before her. "Are you familiar with Section 722-6 of the Penal Law? Do you know what it states?"

"Yes," I said, "I'm familiar with it." It was my trap, not hers, and she had slipped into it too easily.

"Did you observe the defendant violate that section of the Penal Law dealing with jostling—place his hand in close proximity to a woman's pocketbook, which, according to Section 722-6 of the Penal Law, is an offense?"

"Yes, I did."

"Why didn't you arrest him then? For jostling? For the lesser crime, the offense of jostling?"

My voice was hard and flat, my answer anticipated by every police officer in the courtroom. "At the time the defendant committed the act of jostling, there were many other unidentified persons in the immediate vicinity, including several children. My partner and I approached the defendant with the intention of placing him under arrest, but by the time we moved toward him, he had already moved further into the crowd. We didn't want to take any sudden action which might cause harm or injury to an innocent bystander," I recited by rote.

Mrs. Drexel nodded her head, then sharply shook her head from side to side with a kind of weariness rather than anger. Her voice sounded heavy now, and sad. "So you watched him until he committed the *felony,* the act of grand larceny, eh?"

"Yes, ma'am. It was only a second or so later. After he hit the pocketbook, and by the time I finally reached his side, he was in the act of removing a wallet from the right-hand back trouser pocket of Mr. Ludwig, the complainant in this case."

"You're a very cautious police officer, would you say?" The question was contemptuous, the tone insulting.

"Where innocent people are concerned, I . . ."

"Oh, yes, and very slow moving, and so cautious that

you stood back, according to your testimony, and let the defendant get away with an offense so that you could get him for a felony."

I didn't answer.

"I demand to know why you didn't arrest him for the *offense!*"

The district attorney called out from his chair that the officer had taken satisfactory police action and had responded properly to the question, but Mrs. Drexel, in a new burst of indignation, shouted him down with her own accusation. "You decided to give him enough rope, isn't that it?"

And finally, responding now, meeting the anger, I snapped back, "Yes, yes, that's right, Mrs. Drexel, and he hung himself with the rope!"

My answer and Mrs. Drexel's scalding remarks were lost in a crossfire of shouting by the district attorney and the judge. The court stenographer studied his fingernails for a moment, his hands off the keys of his machine.

The rest of the cross-examination was tense and quick. Mrs. Drexel covered the ground already chopped into earlier with my partner, who had testified first, and with the complainant, a befuddled, regretful man who would rather have forgotten the whole thing with the return of his wallet.

"Now, let's discuss the matter of the charge of 1897— possession of a dangerous weapon. When the defendant was searched by your partner, a four-inch knife was found in his trouser pocket, is that correct?"

"It was a switchblade knife, yes," I replied.

"All right. That makes it sound more sinister, doesn't it?"

"I don't know. I think a four-inch blade in the hands of someone like the defendant is pretty sinister, regardless of what you might call it."

She ignored my remarks. "Now, when you put the question to him, the defendant told you, did he not, that the knife was used by him in his job as a packer?"

"No, that wasn't what he said at first. He said that he

didn't know how the knife got there. That it wasn't his knife."

"Did you accuse the defendant of having used the knife in an alleged attack? Wasn't that when he got frightened and said he had never seen the knife before?"

"In questioning the defendant about the knife, I asked him if he had used the knife on a girl, in the park, and then he said that the knife wasn't his."

Mrs. Drexel screwed her face into a look of amazement. "Was a girl attacked in the park previous to this arrest? Did you have any reason to suspect the defendant in such an attack?"

"Mrs. Drexel," I said impatiently, "I wanted to get a statement from the defendant relative to his possession of the knife. First, he said it wasn't his; then, after a few more questions, he told us that he only used it for self-defense, in gang fights or things like that."

The foreman of the jury scowled, and Paco had the misfortune to turn his face toward the jury box at that exact moment. He grinned brightly, and nodded his head up and down, and the foreman of the jury made a snorting noise and shook his head.

"You lied in asking him that question about a girl and an alleged attack. You lied, didn't you?"

I shrugged. "How can a lie take the form of a question? You might say that we tricked him into an admission."

"Yes, I might say that; and I might say that you tricked him into grand larceny, according to your own testimony."

"Go ahead and say it, Mrs. Drexel. The fact is, he committed grand larceny and 1897."

Her scorn matched my own. "Oh, you gave him the business, all right." She muttered the words to herself and, without looking toward him, she waved her hand at the D.A., who was starting to rise. "Oh, save it, Mr. Langton, save it, I'm finished with her. It just sickens me a little, that's all—they are phony charges, both of them. Go ahead, go ahead, Detective Uhnak, you got your grand larceny and your 1897 arrests. Wait. One more question."

Her voice was razor sharp, her eyes glinted coldly. "Do you get credit for two arrests or one?"

I watched her steadily, my voice low and even. "I'll settle for one conviction, Mrs. Drexel."

We regarded each other in a kind of hypnotic glaring, and I could see nothing in the room but the blazing, glinting, enlarged eyes beneath the shining spectacles. Then I stood up from the chair, felt my foot miss the step of the raised platform; I groped for the railing, then turned away from Mrs. Drexel. I walked past her and found space beside my partner.

"Christ," he whispered behind his hand, "is she burning! Look at poor old Minnie, she's fuming!"

Poor old Minnie can drop dead. The questions repeated themselves hollowly in my head, the meanings and insinuations hammering and thundering through me: was he the only Puerto Rican? Didn't he look dirty and out of place, standing there among those nice, clean, respectable people? I felt myself bursting with my unspoken words. It wasn't like that; I'm not like that. I could feel the heat in my cheeks and the cold taste of anger in my mouth.

Mrs. Drexel went to her client's side and bent forward, whispering earnestly into his ear. Paco's head bounced up and down and his face contorted into a puzzled half-smile; then he whispered some words to her, his hand gesticulating vaguely. Mrs. Drexel apparently answered his doubts, for he nodded and seemed to be grinning at some thoughts of his own.

Mrs. Drexel's witnesses included a slim, tall man wearing a light gray suit and tie to match, who was a Mr. Gerstein, Paco's employer. He testified that Paco worked for him as a packer, had been in his employ for four months, earned forty dollars a week and had been a steady and honest worker. He also testified that Paco used his knife for cutting strings and rope and that all the boys used knives for this kind of work. He said that he had nothing bad to say about Paco. And his manner said that he wished he had never heard of Paco.

The district attorney advanced quietly, holding the dan

gerous yellow sheet—Paco's record—in his hand, and asked Mr. Gerstein if he knew that Paco had been convicted twice for jostling. Mr. Gerstein, in honest surprise, said no, he hadn't known that. Then the district attorney asked Mr. Gerstein if he still thought that Paco was an honest boy, and Mr. Gerstein, flustered and greatly agitated, said, "Well, so far as I know." The D.A. smiled and thanked him, and Mr. Gerstein retreated to some dark corner whence he had come, nodding self-consciously as he passed Paco, who was beaming a wide grin in his direction.

Father Fernaldo testified that Paco was a good, quiet boy who attended mass, not at frequent intervals, but occasionally. He said that he lived with some cousins and worked as a packer for a living. As far as he, Father Fernaldo, knew, Paco was a mild, quiet boy. The D.A. passed Father Fernaldo with a friendly wave of his hand —he could afford to be generous. Then he nodded to Mrs. Drexel, but she said stonily, "No further witnesses. Defense rests," and put one hand protectively on Paco's shoulder, unwilling to offer him up to the district attorney.

Within twenty minutes, a stretch-and-cigarette length of time, the jury returned the verdict of guilty on both counts, and Judge Goldhaber glared down at Paco, who listened to the verdict, an empty, dead look on his paling face. The judge's eyebrows crept down across the bridge of his nose, and his mouth made harsh but wordless sounds. Finally, consulting the bridgeman, he set down a date for sentencing. Then he made a short speech to the jury, addressing it mainly to the foreman, who nodded his vigorous agreement. He spoke about society and vicious thieves and thugs and muggers and rat-punks. All the while, Mrs. Drexel's hand rested on Paco's arm, until he pulled it away sharply, with a sudden, bitter, comprehending look on his gray face. When the judge's speech was finished, he motioned brusquely to the court attendant, snarling, "Get him outta here!" Mrs. Drexel began speaking rapidly to Paco, who was being tugged along by the court officer. She patted him on the shoulder, on the arm, nodding her head in a curiously motherly way. Paco would not meet her eyes, and she stood watching him until he disappeared behind the barred doors of the detention room and the large oak door closed again, fitting neatly into the contours of the courtroom.

Outside the courtroom, in the marble corridor, I felt the dry, sick taste of my cigarette deep in my throat, felt the keyed-up excitement that always carried me through a trial. I was sticky and damp with perspiration and felt tired and yet highly elated at the same instant. A deep resentment was knotting my stomach, and I felt the twinges of pain, a sharp pinching sensation high on my right side. The gnawing would subside after a few hours, if I had some tepid milk, munched the chalky pills, stopped smoking. But it was strong right then, and I felt a cold, clammy sweat on my forehead and my hands were trembling.

"Listen," I told my partner, speaking quickly, afraid I was going to be sick. "I want to get washed up. I'll meet you by the water cooler in about ten minutes."

Without hearing his answer, I turned and walked quickly from him. The ladies room was empty. It was a long white tile room with two smeary washbasins, four gray-doored chambers, and a long chrome-framed mirror running the width of the room, over the sinks. I ran the cold water over my wrists, then splashed some water onto my forehead and cheeks, holding a handful against my eyes and sucking some into my mouth. Swishing the cool water in my mouth, against my cheeks and tongue, I tried to think of nothing but the pleasant, fresh, clean sensation, and watched as the water spilled from my open mouth. I scooped up another mouthful and then the door opened and Mrs. Drexel entered the room.

I swallowed the water in a gulp, choking on it, and blotted my face dry with the scratchy paper towels. Mrs. Drexel stood at the sink next to mine and put her pocketbook on the narrow ledge of shelf directly under the mirror. I looked at my own reflection in the mirror, dabbing at the drops of water around my mouth, but my eyes slid irresistibly to Mrs. Drexel's face. Her eyes were surprisingly small without her glasses, and she dug her fingers into them ruthlessly, as though pushing them into the pits of her sockets, forcing weariness back and away. She rubbed her eyeglasses quickly and carelessly with a piece of tissue paper. As she replaced them I turned toward her, and I could see smudges and drops of water across the lenses.

Mrs. Drexel studied me in her direct way, and her eyes filled the entire circle of each lens of the glasses, as though they were painted comic spectacles. Even when she narrowed her eyes, they seemed round. For the moment, neither of us spoke, each of us seeing the other now in this different setting. I was surprised that Mrs. Drexel seemed shorter, that there were lines around the corners of her mouth, that there was a soft covering of middle-aged fat over her neck. But Mrs. Drexel, measuring me, seemed surprised by nothing.

"Oh, I know you, Mrs. Uhnak," she said suddenly, as though continuing a conversation that had been momentarily interrupted. "You are young and bright and very quick, and you sit up there on that witness stand and you think to yourself: 'I'll show her; she won't beat me!' And it's all a game to you—a contest, a battle of wits that you have to win. When you step down, you feel everyone in court watching you, knowing how very clever you are, how very self-assured."

I didn't answer, but I felt my hands trembling and I forced my fingers to flex; then I let my hands fall naturally and unmoving at my side. I pressed the edges of my back teeth together to stifle the pounding in my throat.

"And now you're feeling very triumphant and very pleased with yourself. 'I've beaten the old bag and she's mad as hell, and the hell with her!'" Mrs. Drexel did not pause; her voice was soft, but it had a strong and steady whining quality, and she seemed to be hurrying to get the words out, to get it all said before she was interrupted or out of breath. "You beat me, yes. You got your conviction and you can go back and tell them in your office about how sore poor old Minnie was, and how she came around crying afterward, but let me tell you something!" Mrs. Drexel lowered her voice, and her words were hissing and tense. "You didn't beat me. And you didn't beat the poor little slob of a Spanish boy in there. He was beaten the day before he was born and I was beaten the day after I became an attorney for the Legal Aid. We only get the losers, so you can't beat us. You beat yourself—you all do, all you fresh, bright youngsters, every time you get on that stand, and every time you see it as a game that you have to win, all the way home, regardless of the price someone else has to pay for your victory. You have to win it all, and you don't budge an inch and you don't give an inch!"

"Should I have let him walk away with the man's wallet, Mrs. Drexel?" My voice was hollow in the room, and the sound of it was brittle and unfamiliar.

Mrs. Drexel's face contorted into a flushing, twisting kind of anger. "Oh, don't give me that! Don't insult my intelligence. Don't tell me about you having your job and me having my job. Don't try to con me, Mrs. Uhnak, I've been around too long. I've seen too much of it. I'm reaching you, you know what we're talking about. He faces seven and a half to ten years, and that bastard Goldhaber will give him the max. You know it and so do I. You should never have let him get his hands on the wallet. You should have moved yourself and nabbed him for jostling." Mrs. Drexel inhaled a great gasp of air, holding up her hand to stop me from speaking. She wasn't finished. "Oh, you're a pretty little girl, Mrs. Detective Uhnak, your face is very young and soft. But I'll give you another two years. It will start. The hardness. It shows in your faces, you pretty ones. Yes, in your eyes first, and then in your mouth. In your expression—the bitterness, the cynicism. The rotten hardness and callousness. There is nothing uglier or more grotesque than the face of a once-pretty woman who has turned hard." Mrs. Drexel's mouth twitched, and she looked around quickly, her hands rushing into her pocketbook for something, digging impatiently, then she snapped the clasp again. "I know you," she whispered, more to herself than to me.

It had touched a nerve center, a raw, living, painful nerve center that Mrs. Drexel had not imagined. I know you. All my life I had dreaded that kind of identity—one of them, one of those, I know you. I felt the color drain from my face, licked my lips drily, and Mrs. Drexel looked up, saw my face, narrowed her eyes shrewdly.

"Oh? You don't like that? You don't think it's true about you? You're different? Ha!" she snorted contemptuously.

I felt an urgency to justify myself, to identify myself. But why? To whom? To this woman with her unknowing opinions? When I answered, it was with resentful words rather than with the other sentiments that were pounding inside of me. "Look, Mrs. Drexel, do you want me to cry about a little crook named Paco? He'd be the first to laugh if I did. He'd be the first to laugh at you and your great concern."

The words hit the woman, and she blinked rapidly and I knew I had wounded her. "Go ahead," I said, "if you want to knock your head against a stone wall, go ahead. Not me."

It wasn't what I had wanted to say. I had wanted to tell her something else, to start somewhere else, but our beginning had been out there, in the courtroom. It was the smug, knowing, arrogant expression on the woman's face that had forced these hard words. This beat-up, soft, old bleeding heart!

As my mind formed the words, I gasped inwardly. My God, my God. It isn't me thinking like this; it isn't me speaking to her this way.

"Oh, it's a stone wall all right, and I bang away and I chip away." Mrs. Drexel's hand touched her dark, disheveled hair without purpose. "The walls in prison are stone walls too, and they don't move much either when you beat them with your fists. Do you know that boy you're sending to prison? Do you know Paco?"

I raised my eyes to the ceiling and sighed a long, insulting, annoyed sound.

"Oh, sure, you know him. He's a little gutter rat and he's got two others on the sheet, and you're right. That's all he is, a little, dirty, smelly, Spic gutter rat."

"Listen here, Mrs. Drexel . . ."

"Oh, I apologize," Mrs. Drexel said with elaborate sarcasm. "You wouldn't call him a 'Spic.' Well, forgive me then. The word just slipped out and maybe it isn't part of your vernacular. A little Puerto Rican rat, then. But let me tell you something: he was born a baby, a little brown, unwanted bastard, and his mother left him with *her* mother along with an assortment of little brown-ish-whitish-blackish bastards while she ran off to get herself fixed up with a couple more of the same. The grandmother threw them out when they could walk, and they learned how to steal food, how to steal bread, and how to steal anything they could get their little hands on, because the poor, stupid little bastards, God help them, they wanted to live. Don't ask me why—the eternal mystery of life—but they wanted to live and they managed. Barely. Paco came here when he was twelve years old to find his mother, all by himself, with just the clothes on his back. He found her and she looked at her skinny, runty, blotchy little son and told him to get the hell out and leave her alone. So he went to live with some cousins and they took him in and he slept on the fire escape in the summer and shared a very full, very busy bed in the winter. They told him to eat somewhere else, because they had enough trouble feeding their own kids. Oh, blink at me, Mrs. Uhnak, blink hard, it doesn't matter, does it, because Paco is a scummy little bum, and you're right, because he is, and he'd steal your eye teeth if you opened your mouth!"

Listening to the flow of words that came from the woman without ceasing, I cried inwardly—but not to Mrs. Drexel. I know Paco, that inward voice said, I worked with him in the settlement house for over a year, only his name wasn't Paco, it was Luis. He was eight years old, and he had a large open gash over his eye one day and he told me his father had thrown a shoe at him. And he didn't tell me with any sense of outrage: it was a thing his father did when he was drunk or angry or just felt like it. I took Luis to the hospital, and the doctor sewed him up, without any anesthetic, just took stitches in the child's head, and said, "These people are like pigs!" Luis just sat there, not saying a word, not making a sound, with this doctor jabbing him and saying these things. I bought Luis an ice cream soda because his world was so intolerable and I didn't know what to do for him, and he beamed like he was the luckiest boy in the world. He was proud of his stitches and I felt ripped up inside.

I know Paco, all right. But you don't know me and you have no right to judge me.

Then finally when I did speak, the words were not the ones I wanted to say. Again it was the cold voice of the stranger—the words and tone forced from me by the accusations of this blazing and righteous little woman. "Mrs. Drexel, why didn't you plead him guilty, cop out to petit larceny and let the probation officer write up Paco's history? It's been done before. Why did you go to trial?" And then, cruelly sensing that I had hit into the woman's soft center, I twisted the words for some revenge. "Or didn't you want to give Judge Goldhaber the satisfaction? Maybe you have your own game to play."

Mrs. Drexel clutched her pocketbook with both hands and slammed it against the sink. "Oh, no," she said, moaning, "oh, no, you won't question my motives. I won't permit that. We try, that's all, we try. The boy insisted on his innocence, and I won't plead a boy under those circumstances."

The woman's face had the weary, heavy pallor of a prisoner. She had spent too many years inside the walls, within walls of her own making—living it, breathing it, sleeping it. She spoke with the driving, repetitive quality of the attorney to the unknown, the unwanted, the hopeless. Mrs. Drexel never had a winner. When she spoke o her clients, the words fell on deaf or scheming ears. She knew they were all liars and cheaters and thieves and degenerates and criminals and that they had no love for her and would use her and turn on her and scorn her. And all the years of talking to them and telling them and ghting for them had taken a heavy toll. The woman carried the burden within her, without hope of any kind, and was streaked and drawn into her face, and it sounded in er voice.

"Mrs. Drexel," I said softly, feeling the pity and sadness and guilt that had been beneath all of my feelings toward this woman, "I'm an officer of the law, and you're an officer of the court. We have laws for people to live by and we have a system of laws and"—I waved my hand in the air, groping for a word—"and justice!"

Mrs. Drexel drew in her breath and seemed to revive and snap back into life fully. "Ah, yes," she said, "ah, yes. Justice." She said the word carefully, snapping her lips together and nodding her head. She leaned against the edge of the sink, not noticing that the rim was wet and soapy and was staining the side of her skirt. "Let me tell you about justice, Mrs. Uhnak, let me tell you all about 'justice.' "

I flipped the crumpled piece of wet paper towel which I had been holding all the while into the wastebasket with an impatient gesture and shook my head. "Not today, Mrs. Drexel, my partner is waiting for me."

"No," the woman said as I started to leave, "for just a moment." There was a strange, almost pleading sound in her words. Wanting to leave this room, to be far away from Mrs. Drexel and her crazy, magnified eyes, I could not move.

"Justice." Mrs. Drexel repeated the word, but this time in a harsh and grating voice. "Justice is depicted, traditionally, as being blind: a tall, clean, solid woman holding a scale before her, weighing the facts, blinded to prejudice or distraction of any kind. The facts, yes. No mitigating circumstances—just weighing the facts against the necessities of the law. We teach all our young law students, and yes, all our young police officers, that this is a good and fine thing, and as it should be. Blind justice. But let me tell you," Mrs. Drexel's voice rose shrilly now perhaps to her own surprise, for it echoed in the tile room and bounced off the walls, and she lowered her voice but it was still emotional and ragged and trembled slightly, "let me tell you, justice should not be a blindfolded woman. Justice should be round-eyed, clear-eyed and deep-seeing, looking beyond the man standing there front of the court to be judged for the one, particul crime. Justice should see into his life and into all the things that have touched him, and been done to him, and twisted him into what he is—all the hurts and hungers and deprivations that have built him into what he is."

Mrs. Drexel was seeing all the Pacos of her lifetime; there was an almost unbearable look of pain and anguish and misery on her features, burning from her eyes. She twisted her body slightly, as though warding off a pain she herself was inflicting, yet was powerless to stop. "Justice, ha? It has no meaning, it does not exist. Not in our courts, not in our lives. Justice isn't either one of those things, Mrs. Uhnak—it's not blind and impartial, not all-seeing and pitying. The eye of justice is jagged!"

Mrs. Drexel shook her head up and down briskly, and it was as though the thought had just occurred to her and she seemed amazed at how clear and true her own words were. "Yes, that's it. Jagged. As jagged as broken glass. Sharp and cruel and distorted, seeing things cruelly, without pity, judging on the instant, isolated deed and judging the deed, condemning the man. Justice is the political instrument of a clown-magistrate who convulsed them in Night Court for years and reads his reviews in the columns like an entertainer and who gauges what kind of day in court he's had by the number of laughs he's gotten. Now. Now, then. How does that seem to you, eh?"

I ran my tongue over my parched lips, but my tongue was dry and sticky. The woman looked so anguished and pain-racked. The strength and power and vitality seemed to have deserted her again. I saw that the left side of her skirt was stained with water and the liquid green soap, and I pointed to the wet spot and said, "Your . . . skirt. It's wet, Mrs. Drexel."

She stared at me, bewildered, as though the words were spoken in an unknown language, and I pointed. She looked down absently. "Oh. Oh, yes, it got wet, didn't it." Her voice was low and distracted, and she began rubbing the stain with her fingers in a futile, undirected effort. I offered her a clean handkerchief.

"I think you'd better wet the handkerchief and try to rub the soap out. It will stain."

"Yes. Yes, of course." Mrs. Drexel soaked the handkerchief under the cold water and began rubbing it into the stain, which spread blackly over her left thigh. Then she blotted it a few times with the dry half of the handkerchief, which she then bunched up and handed to me, saying, "It's wet. I'm sorry."

The abrupt, complete change in conversation made me feel dizzy and lightheaded. The room was damp and Mrs. Drexel looked like someone I had never seen before, someone puzzled and at a loss over a soapy stain on her skirt. "It doesn't matter," I said, putting the soggy ball into my pocketbook.

"No, you're right. It doesn't matter, does it?" Mrs. Drexel's words were not for a wet handkerchief. They were weary, exhausted, defeated words, said more to herself, to her own thoughts. A deep, involuntary intake of air hit the back of the woman's throat and emerged in a soft sigh. She glanced at herself in the mirror, moved her hand in a fussy gesture over her hair, missing the stray lock that stuck out over the rim of her eyeglasses. "It doesn't matter," she repeated.

"Mrs. Drexel," I called to her, not knowing what it was I wanted to say.

"Yes?" She turned, her face alert again, bright again, the strain miraculously receding.

"Mrs. Drexel, I want you to know that . . . well, that I admire you. And I respect your feelings. But . . . well, we each have our job to do."

"Yes, we each have our job to do." Her voice was flat as though in disappointment, as though she had been expecting to hear some other words.

I glanced in the mirror, turned my face sideways, dabbed the edge of my chin with my finger, licked m' lips and walked past Mrs. Drexel, who stood watchin, me. My hand on the doorknob, I turned as Mrs. Drexe made some slight motion, some slight sound. She wa facing me.

"Mrs. Uhnak, I'm . . . I'm tired today." She faltere for the first time, then laughed a short, bitter, humorles sound. "*Today*. I think, Mrs. Uhnak, that you are prot ably a very nice girl and a very hard-working girl and a very earnest girl. I think you probably take your job quite seriously, and that is a good thing. But," she said, raising her finger, her voice hoarse, "these are human beings we deal with here. They are human beings when you get them, and when I get them, with many years of their lives over and done with. Don't lose sight of that fact, my dear young lady. Not ever!"

I nodded, made some sound, as a child would answer an old, dominating teacher whom she admired with one part of herself, yet pitied and feared, all at the same time.

I left Mrs. Drexel standing before the mirror, poking absently at her face. My partner was leaning against the wall in the corridor, beside the water fountain, smoking and reading his crumpled morning *News*. He dropped the cigarette under his large shoe when he saw me coming toward him.

"I was wondering what happened. I saw poor old Minnie going in there after you. She fight the war all over again?" He laughed a short, mean sound.

"No," I answered, not looking at him. "I didn't speak to her. She was washing her face—we just ignored each other."

He laughed again. "You sure beat the pants off her today."

I looked at him curiously, seeing his smile, noticing the lean cheeks, the narrow, hard, joyless eyes. "Yes," I said softly, "I sure beat poor old Minnie, didn't I?"

And I didn't speak about the case any more nor about Minnie Drexel, for we were, after all, kin. She was trying to buy, with her life, what I had tried to purchase for one hundred and twenty-five dollars.

Epilogue

Just recently, a lieutenant who knew me during my initial days in police work was reflecting on his first thoughts of me. "Dot," he said, "you were a starry-eyed idealist, always expecting the best from people and always shocked when they didn't come up to your expectations. I had you marked as a born social worker." And then he laughed and said, thoughtfully, "And I don't think you've changed a bit!"

His remark was offered as a curious kind of compliment, for an idealist with deep feelings about people has a difficult time of it in police work. His evaluation of me as "not having changed a bit" was wrong, and I have been trying to measure some of the changes that have taken place as a result of my career in police work. I can look back from the vantage point of having been removed from active police field work for several years now, and perhaps I can view myself somewhat more objectively than would be possible otherwise. It is interesting to note that I have been accused, by newer acquaintances, of being a very cynical person, and I have been weighing the two evaluations in an attempt to arrive at some conclusions.

What the lieutenant said about my always expecting the best from people and being shocked when they let me down was true to some extent. When I was very young I was a perfectionist, driving myself toward certain ideals and I measured others against my own standards. I expected people to be and to behave in my own image of perfection. Certainly I have matured to the level where I feel a responsibility for my own actions but a realiz.

tion that I have no right to judge others. This was a long and hard lesson to learn, and a tremendously important fact to accept. I have come to be a realist about people and have learned through personal experience that some very good people are capable of some very bad deeds and some very bad people are capable of some very good deeds. I have learned that human beings are the most complicated creatures existent. Where once I had believed we were each given two choices, to follow the good road or to follow the bad road, I now know that life leads us along endlessly criss-crossing, spiraling, twisting paths, tangling into a network of directions not easily definable nor separable. Where once I had believed that an individual human being had free choice to plan and follow his destiny, I now realize that we are all under many pressures, from within and from without, that lead us into actions and directions *almost* beyond our control, and that our ability to lead our lives as decent human beings is often something greater than a small triumph.

If I am indeed cynical, it is only because I have learned to look truly into the "systems" that govern our lives. I do not believe the pious, pompous words carved into the buildings where "justice" is announced; I do not believe that justice is administered as it should be—fairly and fully. Yet, I have become mature enough to believe that we have the best system that man has been able to devise—be it far from perfect. I know that justice does not exist in our daily lives, and I have learned that life is not a system of rewards and punishments meted out to us as an inevitable result of our accomplishments.

Yet, I am not truly a cynic, for I still expect that we will one day all be better than we are. I believe that we continually make progress as human beings and that though we inch forward almost imperceptibly, we will one day come to know each other and make greater attempts to understand and accept each other. My lifelong enemy, as a young girl and still now, as a grown woman, has been the bitter generalization, the tossed-out, all-inclusive remark that marks and scars and stains vast groups of people indiscriminately. I questioned these generalizations as a young girl almost instinctively, and I deplore them now as a grown woman from years of experience with vast numbers of people from all backgrounds.

If I have acquired a certain skepticism and a certain hardness, it was a necessary growing process, for a police officer cannot be a sponge absorbing the misery and degradation he encounters. But on the other hand, he cannot let his inevitable shell become anything more than that. He cannot let the hardness penetrate to the center of him, or he will cease to be a human being.

If through the years I have been shocked or disillusioned or sickened by the people I have encountered, or the situations in which I have become involved, I do not now regret my career, for I feel my life in police work has been a tremendously important education.

My career has given me a backlog of stories—interesting, amusing, offbeat, terrifying—so that I am able to entertain a group of listeners. But this is not the important thing.

In the inevitable quiet moments, when I am alone, I am able now to evaluate my growth in understanding, tolerance and acceptance, not only of others, but of myself, and to realize my responsibilities as a human being.

This is the important thing.